Jane Austen's

The Sense and Sensibility Companion

Includes Study Guide, Historical Context, Biography, and Character Index

BookCaps™ Study Guides

www.bookcaps.com

Cover Image © ultramarin - Fotolia.com

Table of Contents

Historical Context

Jane Austen is a celebrated and much loved English novelist who primarily wrote romance novels. Some of her most famous work includes <u>Pride and Prejudice</u>, <u>Sense & Sensibility</u> and <u>Emma</u>. Her work chiefly concerns the lives of the landed gentry—the wealthy families of the upper classes. It is her exploration of contemporary social issues within these families and stories that have made her stories extremely popular. She was a fairly popular author at the time, but only experienced enormous success after her death. Due to publishing anonymously, Jane was an unknown author, but she was celebrated among the upper classes especially. By the 20th Century, she was known by name and generally celebrated as one of the renowned English novelists.

Austen was born in December 1775 and died at the age of 41 in 1817. She was a member of an upper class family who were close. She did not have much fortune to speak of, however, which often prevented her from making a marriage match. She was only engaged once, but on accepting, she realized she had made a complete mistake and rejected the man in question the following day. Although not much biographical information is available for Austen, historians know that she was educated by her father and brother on returning from school, and they supported her writing. She had six brothers and one other sister. Jane Austen started to feel sick, and her health deteriorated quickly, but she continued to work on her writing until she was confined to her bed. Austen was unmarried when she died.

Austen's earliest writing projects were for her family's own amusement, not for publication. Most of these pieces of work, including an epistolary novel, are lost—either destroyed by Austen herself or by other family members. Austen frequently destroyed letters she wrote, and those that were not destroyed by her hand were either censored or destroyed by her sister, Cassandra.

Austen began to write the manuscript for <u>Sense and Sensibility</u> as a series of letters between the two sisters when she was 19. It was called <u>Elinor and Marianne.</u> <u>Sense and Sensibility</u>, as you can probably guess by the title, was reworked from this previous project into a narrative novel with a philosophical attitude. Austen appeared to start the novel with an aim to argue that sense was the most advantageous ability, but by the end seemed to either change her mind or forget her original aim. Marianne and Willoughby are drawn to one another because of their vanity and over the top emotion. They do not stop to consider the affect their behaviour had on other people. As a result, their relationship failed. Edward and Elinor, on the other hand, are conservative with their emotions. They conceal what they need to and protect those around them. They do love one another, however, and it is this love that helps them get through the tougher times. As Willoughby is generally forgiven for his behaviour, and that Marianne succeeds in love and is a well liked character, it is unclear if sense or sensibility certainly triumphed at all. In fact, it appears that both of these traits must co-exist in order for these characters to survive.

Plot Overview

Short Synopsis

Elinor and Marianne Dashwood are forced to leave their home and go to a Cottage in a new county with the rest of their family. The novel follows their trials and triumphs in love and explores whether reason or emotion in love are the best approaches.

Detailed Synopsis

After Mr. Henry Dashwood dies and leaves all of his money to his first wife's son, John, his second wife and three daughters are without a home and little money. Mrs. Dashwood, Elinor, Marianne and Margaret are made strangers in their own home, Norland Park, and eventually have to leave it to John and Fanny Dashwood. Elinor is sad to leave Norland, particularly, because she and Fanny's brother, Edward Ferrars, have become close. The entire family believe she and Edward might end up engaged to marry. One of Mrs. Dashwood's relatives offer them Barton Cottage as their new home, and they leave Norland Park forever.

Once they arrive at Barton, Mrs. Dashwood's relative, Sir John Middleton, and Mrs. Jennings become their new friends and take up all of the Dashwood's time by throwing parties and dinners. Lady Middleton is not an affectionate woman and spends most of her time repeating the same things. Mrs. Jennings and Sir John, however, take sheer delight in amusing themselves. They tease a new friend, Colonel Brandon, about his affection for Marianne. Marianne is not pleased at all: Colonel Brandon is old and incapable of falling in love again. Marianne is convinced that a person can only fall in love once and are unable to have a second chance. They also tease Elinor about the mysterious Mr. F she is reportedly in love with. Edward does not visit them as he promised to do so, and Elinor is worried.

Marianne goes out for a walk in the rain one day with Margaret and twists her ankle. John Willoughby, a charming and handsome man, rushes to her aid and carries Marianne back inside the cottage. Marianne admires Willoughby for his cultured soul and his outspoken nature. Elinor tries to warn Marianne to be more polite and less open with her feelings, but Marianne thinks Elinor wants her to be cold—the way she thinks Elinor is. Elinor and Mrs. Dashwood soon suspect that Willoughby and Marianne are engaged to be married, but neither have the courage to say something. After organizing a picnic on some grounds, Brandon is called away on urgent business when he receives a letter. Both Willoughby and Marianne are unkind to him, and Mrs. Jennings suggests it is due to a secret Brandon has. When Willoughby suggests he would like to speak to Marianne alone one day, the entire family expect him to propose to her. They return to find Marianne in tears and Willoughby serious. He tells the family he has to go to London for business, and because of Mrs. Smith—the woman who holds his fortune in her hands. Marianne descends into a deep sorrow.

Edward Ferrars finally pays a visit to the family at the Cottage and all are concerned by the change in his behaviour. Elinor thinks he is sad, which worries her. Elinor considers that time has rid him of his feelings for her and tries to hide her heartache from her family to spare them any pain.

Mrs. Jennings invites the Steele sisters to Barton Park. They are cousins of the Middleton family and are therefore relations of both the Dashwoods and her own. Lucy and Anne Steele are both quite impolite, but Lucy tries her best to reign Anne in when she oversteps the mark. Anne talks incessantly and drops hints about various men she likes. Lucy is a sweeter woman by far, but Elinor does not care for either of them because of their openness. One day, Lucy visits Elinor to confide in her that she has been engaged to marry Edward for the past four years. Elinor tries not to react, but Lucy can tell that something has upset her. Although Elinor does not believe her at first, Lucy presents various pieces of evidence to support her claim. Elinor hides her heartache because she has to promise not to tell anyone about the secret engagement. She tries to speak to Lucy about the engagement on another day to insist that she was only in shock, and not angry with Lucy so that she doesn't suspect her of being in love with Edward. Lucy is overjoyed and tries to talk to Elinor about him every moment they are alone together. Elinor realizes why Edward's behaviour was so changeable, and does not blame him for it. In fact, she pities Edward for being trapped in a loveless engagement because of his honourable nature.

Mrs. Jennings invites Marianne and Elinor to London. Although Elinor does not want to go because she does not want to bump into Edward, Marianne is eager to see Willoughby again. When they arrive, Marianne writes letters to Willoughby to tell him that they have arrived and that he should visit them. He visits the house, but only once when they are out. He does not reply to her letters. Marianne is extremely anxious for a reply and watches for Willoughby when she is forced to go out. Colonel Brandon, who is also in London, reveals to Elinor that everyone in society is discussing the impending marriage between Willoughby and Marianne. Elinor assures him that nothing has been confirmed, even if it is being spoken of as common knowledge. Mrs. Jennings and Elinor persuade Marianne to attend a large party with them where they bump into a weirdly behaved Mr. Willoughby. Willoughby treats them with indifference and coldness as if they had only met a few times before. Marianne begs him to tell her what is wrong, but Willoughby turns away and continues to talk to the noble lady he is with. Marianne grows ill, and the others take her back to Mrs. Jennings' house. Marianne descends into depression and writes to Willoughby the next morning asking him to explain his behaviour. She receives a letter back from him which suggests she had read more into their friendship than he had. He sends Marianne's letters and her lock of hair back. Elinor manages to get an hysterical Marianne to tell her that there was never a formal engagement or understanding between them but that Willoughby had hinted at it. Mrs. Jennings returns to the house after her visits. She, too, has discovered that Willoughby is engaged to the rich Miss Grey. She thinks he is a villain, particularly as he took Marianne to what might have been her future home so that she could look at it. Out of sympathy, Colonel Brandon visits them at Mrs. Jennings' home to tell Elinor about Willoughby's past. He seduced Brandon's fifteen year old ward, Eliza, and then left her to fend for herself after she became pregnant. Elinor thinks Marianne is lucky to have escaped him.

Fanny has invited the Steele sisters to her home in London to insult Elinor and Marianne, who—as family— should have been invited to stay before the Steeles. Mrs. Jennings' time was taken up with visits to her new grandson and Mrs. Palmer, her daughter, which meant the Dashwoods were often at Mrs. Jennings' home alone. Lucy thinks it means Fanny likes her, which gives her hope that Mrs. Ferrars will also accept her when the engagement is no longer a secret. Anne reveals Lucy's secret to Mrs. Ferrars because she is so confident of their position in the family, but Mrs. Ferrars grows hysterical. She throws both Steele sisters out of the house and disowns Edward after he refuses to break off the engagement and marry Miss Morton, a Lord's daughter, instead. He is no longer the heir to the Ferrars fortune and, as far as Mrs. Ferrars is concerned, is no longer her son. Edward's brother, Robert, who is vain and self-important, is now the heir to the fortune. When the news of the engagement reaches the Dashwoods and Mrs. Jennings, Marianne is concerned about Elinor. Elinor reveals she has known about the engagement for many months already because Lucy confided in her, and Marianne insults her for her lack of feeling. Elinor assures her she felt as much pain as Marianne did, but she could not show it, and she had not lost her pride in Edward. He has acted honourably, unlike Willoughby. Colonel Brandon offers Edward a position at the Delaford Parsonage as long as he returned to Oxford to receive his religious orders. Elinor is thankful.

Marianne hears about Willoughby's marriage taking place and becomes depressed. She wants to go back home to their mother, but Elinor persuades her to travel alongside the Palmers and Mrs. Jennings to Cleveland House. It would be a much more comfortable and cheaper journey to take to Cleveland, and then only a day to Barton Cottage after that. Marianne reluctantly agrees. Their journey to Cleveland House is entirely without incident and Marianne is happy she has the freedom to walk around the countryside again. She decides to go walking every day but the weather turns out to be wet and cold. Marianne ends up with a fever which threatens her life. The Palmers flee with their newborn child to another house while the Doctor and Elinor look after Marianne. Colonel Brandon, who arrived at Cleveland shortly after, offers to fetch Mrs. Dashwood after Marianne asks for her. Elinor fears her mother might not reach them in time and worries that she delayed alerting her to Marianne's true condition. Mrs. Jennings believes that Marianne's illness stems from her disappointment in Willoughby, and Elinor agrees. Thankfully, Marianne manages to pull through her fever and begins to rest. Elinor thinks Colonel Brandon and her mother have arrived when she hears a carriage pull up to the door, but when she enters the drawing room it is actually Willoughby.

Willoughby explains he wanted to clear his name a little in case Marianne died believing he was the worst kind of villain. He truly loved Marianne, but was threatened with losing his inheritance if he did not do as Mrs. Smith wanted. Due to his expensive lifestyle and his worry that he might not be able to wait until Mrs. Smith died to get his fortune, he decided he had to marry for money. Elinor pities him because he did love Marianne, but still thinks he acted improperly. He asks for her forgiveness and for her to tell Marianne what he had to say. Elinor will. Colonel Brandon and Mrs. Dashwood finally arrive, and they are relieved that Marianne has survived. Mrs. Dashwood takes care of Marianne, and reveals to Elinor that Colonel Brandon has admitted his love for Marianne. While she has not promised Marianne to him, she has suggested to him that it would make her happy. Elinor knows that only Marianne's acceptance of him would make Brandon happy. When Marianne is well enough, the Dashwoods leave for Barton Cottage. Marianne is still quite weak and cries when she sees Barton because it reminds her of Willoughby. Elinor is proud of her because Marianne is trying hard to appear cheerful and to not willingly descend into hysterics like she did in the past. While on a small walk, Marianne talks to Elinor about Willoughby and wishes she knew the truth about him and if he genuinely loved her. While Elinor debates telling Marianne what Willoughby had said, Marianne admits that her conduct was poor. She was unkind to many people and too open with her feelings. She wishes she had been more like Elinor. Elinor tells her what Willoughby said, and Marianne grows silent and sad, but kisses her sister with gratitude. Mrs. Dashwood is happy she can pity Willoughby a little more than she dislikes him, but knows she can never invite him into their circle of friends again because of the insult to Marianne. Marianne tries her hardest to not let this new news get to her and admits she would never have been happy with Willoughby, especially when she would have found out all of his secrets.

One day, the Dashwood's servant reveals that Mr. Ferrars and Lucy Steele have been married. He saw them in a carriage. Elinor, Marianne and Mrs. Dashwood are a little upset. Elinor wondered how Edward was doing, and whether or not he had received his orders yet. When a gentleman on horseback arrived at the cottage, Elinor assumed it was Colonel Brandon and was happy she would be able to hear news of Edward from him. However, it was actually Edward Ferrars. Elinor and the others tried to keep calm. After Elinor asks after Mrs. Lucy Ferrars, his wife, Edward corrects her—she means Robert's wife. Elinor leaves the room and cries because she is so happy. Edward leaves for a moment and then returns a few hours later to propose to Elinor, his sole reason for returning to Barton. She accepts him, and Mrs. Dashwood approves the match. Edward reveals he received a letter from Lucy suggesting that Edward had fallen in love with someone else. She did not want to marry someone whose heart belonged elsewhere, and so decided to marry Robert. Elinor thinks she changed brothers to gain the fortune, and wondered what Mrs. Ferrars would do on finding out that Robert had done the same thing she had disowned Edward for.

John Dashwood revealed that Mrs. Ferrars had effectively disowned Robert and that Lucy would never be one of her daughters even if she forgave him. He suggested that Edward might need to write to the family to ask for their forgiveness. Edward would not as he did not believe he had done anything wrong, but Elinor persuades him that he had and would need to ask for forgiveness. He decided to go to London, which he does following a small visit from Colonel Brandon.

Edward manages to gain Mrs. Ferrars' forgiveness and then reveals his engagement to Elinor. She is not pleased, but accepts the engagement after considering what happened last time. She gives Edward a little extra money for his income, but not much. It's enough that Elinor and Edward can live from, however, and they are happy. They are married in Autumn and are settled in the Parsonage a month after that. The Dashwoods visited often, particularly as Mrs. Dashwood wanted to encourage the engagement between Marianne and Colonel Brandon. John and Fanny also visited and revealed what had happened when Robert and Lucy came back to London. After asking to be forgiven, Robert was accepted back into the family. Lucy was also forgiven and ended up one of Mrs. Ferrars closest friends. Elinor thought it was silly that Robert was welcomed back with open arms, but Edward assured her that Robert had always been the favourite. They discovered that after Robert had visited Lucy to ask her to break off the engagement, they had met many more times after that. Lucy had always insisted she needed one more conversation to persuade her to break the engagement, and by the time they had realized what had happened, Lucy and Robert were to be married. Robert was pleased he had tricked his brother out of a wife, and they ran away to be married in secret.

After a while, Marianne and Colonel Brandon were married to one another. Marianne loved him as much as she had once loved Colonel Brandon, and Brandon was as happy as he had ever been. Marianne and Elinor liked living so close to one another, and Brandon and Edward remained close friends.

Themes/Motifs

Secrets

There are a few different kind of secrets that are kept in <u>Sense and Sensibility</u>. First, there is the subject of the secret engagement between Edward and Lucy, which takes everyone by surprise and ruffles many feathers. Then, there is the secret of Brandon's ward, Eliza, who Willoughby seduced and abandoned. These are secrets that concern the past lives of the characters and are slowly revealed over time and have a big affect on the narrative of the novel.

Elinor keeps her feelings fairly secret. She does not openly reveal her love for Edward, and she keeps her emotions in check when she is told about his engagement to Lucy—a distinct opposite to Marianne at the party with Willoughby. These secrets make the characters' lives more difficult; although general respect and politeness suggests that they should be kept to maintain their position in polite society, there is a tendency to ask what else a character might be hiding if they manage to hide this much. Austen seems to be commenting on the hypocritical nature of society: they can act polite and proper, but underneath they are anything but.

Sense

Elinor, Edward, Lady Middleton, and Colonel Brandon are some of the novel's most sensible characters. They put others before their own needs because that is what is expected of them, and make sure they do not let emotion guide their every move. Elinor is accused of being cold and unfeeling by Marianne, who cannot believe that she did not react with hysteria when she found out that Edward was already secretly engaged. Elinor protected herself and her family by not causing a scene even though it caused her considerable pain to hide her feelings. Although Elinor is fairly reserved, she still loves deeply. She cares for her sisters, mother, and for Edward. It is sense that allows her to moderate her feelings in public.

Sensibility

Revealing emotions and acting impulsively is explored through the characters of Willoughby, Marianne, Charlotte Palmer and Mrs. Jennings, to name but a few. Willoughby seduces Eliza without thinking about the consequences and leaves her to fend for herself. He is open about his feelings for Marianne with no real guilt, even though he knows he has no plans to marry her. Marianne is also emotionally open: she descends into hysterics, almost faints in public, insults her friends behind their backs and descends into a deep depression which almost kills her. Both Elinor and Marianne represent the polar opposites of sense and sensibility, and they have to learn from one another to survive the trials they are put through and end up happily married. Marianne has to admit to herself that her behaviour was impolite and incorrect before she can start to come to terms with what happened between her and Willoughby, and it is this sensible, reasonable behaviour which allows her to survive.

The Home

The loss of Norland Park is a devastating blow for the Dashwood family—not only are they made homeless, they also lose the place they cherish the most. Marianne walks around it worrying who will enjoy the trees and both she and Mrs. Dashwood cry when they finally have to leave. When Marianne is in thick of her depression after finding out about Willoughby's marriage, she longs to go back home, and when she becomes sick she can only think about the delay back home that her illness has incurred. It is a place of comfort, warmth and where both family and friends gather. It is the place Marianne vows never to leave again, and, even though she marries Colonel Brandon and leaves Barton Cottage, she has a home of her own to look after by the end.

A home can also reflect the economic well-being and social standing of the family who live within it. The Dashwoods are upset that they will have to give up their fine home to move into a smaller and poorer looking cottage, and Mrs. Dashwood worries about making improvements to it to make it look larger as soon as she enters it.

Fortunes

Money makes people do strange things, and the world of Sense and Sensibility is no different. Willoughby, for example, gives up his love for Marianne to marry someone with a fortune so that he can continue spending as much as he has been. That he discovers after the marriage that Mrs. Smith would have allowed him to marry Marianne and still receive his fortune had he acted with honour is an ironic note. Willoughby allows himself to be blinded and obsessed with money that it controls his judgement and actions.

Lucy swaps Ferrars brothers when Edward loses his inheritance, despite the fact that they had been secretly engaged for the past four years. Her love for Edward was meant to be great, but it disappeared as soon as his fortune did.

Honourable Behaviour

Colonel Brandon and Edward both act with honour and are generally celebrated for it in society. Brandon protects his young ward, Eliza, after she is cruelly treated by Willoughby. He stands by her and does not abandon her. Edward stands by Lucy after the engagement is discovered even though it means losing his whole family and his inheritance. He gave everything up for her because it was the right thing to do, not because he still loved her. Willoughby, on the other hand, left Eliza to fend for herself after he seduced her. Although he argued that Eliza could have left the Inn without him having to give her instructions to do so, it's a cold excuse for treating a young girl poorly. His second offence concerning Marianne is generally well known in society, and most friends of the Dashwood family ignore him after it. Despite this, he is pitied by Elinor and Marianne once they discover he actually did love Marianne after all, and lives a fairly happy life. It could be that Austen wanted to point out the hypocritical reactions both characters and audiences had towards romantic heroes and that they could get away with much more.

Gender Roles

The relationship between Edward and Elinor is an intriguing one. Elinor is the more dominant partner out of the two which is traditionally the male role, particularly during Austen's time. Edward is far more submissive and insecure. The same can be seen in the marriage between John and Fanny Dashwood. Fanny does not overtly question her husband's behaviour but uses manipulation and cunning to get her own way—this means she controls her husband. Austen's female characters have always been strong, but these characters seem to suggest that women were far more aware of what was going on which gave them an edge. John has no idea he is being manipulated, and Edward often has to be told what to do; for example, Elinor tells Edward he does have to ask for his family's forgiveness after he initially refuses to do so. This eventually leads to a reconciliation between him and his family, and consent for his engagement to Elinor.

Love and Suffering

Love and pain go hand in hand, and it is certainly no different in the world of Sense and Sensibility. All of the new couples suffer in some way; Elinor because Edward is already engaged, Marianne because Willoughby rejects her, and Colonel Brandon because Marianne does not seem to care one bit about him. Austen takes the position that many do: that to achieve real love and happiness, there is quite a bit of danger involved. Some couples will not make it for various reasons, but some do and the struggle is worth it in the end.

Social Status

Social rank dictates whom can marry whom, and whether or not families will see the match as an ideal and valuable one, or as a poor match. Both Lucy and Elinor are poor matches because they have no fortunes of their own. Miss Morton and Miss Grey are considered more valuable because they have fortunes to their name. Likewise, Lucy wants to remain engaged to Edward despite the loss of his fortune because she hopes something good will come his way. He is, after all, a gentleman. She climbs ranks in society by marrying Robert and becomes the close friend of Mrs. Ferrars even after being told she is inferior. Personal feelings—love, for example—are often ignored in favour of climbing rank because more opportunities are available to those higher up. As a contrast, Eliza—who was left without a penny to her name—could not leave the Inn where she was abandoned and was all by herself. Her mother, in a similar situation, died because Colonel Brandon's brother sent her away without any money.

Marriage

Marriage, as ever, is the end goal for daughters and sons. Parents, and older friends of the family, want to see their young charges married off and married *well*. Mrs. Jennings declares that she will see either one or both of the older Dashwood sisters married off to good suitors as she has already done so with her children. It is her immediate goal. Likewise, Mrs. Dashwood wants to ensure that Colonel Brandon and Marianne will end up married and invites Brandon to stay with them, and travels to Delaford to stay with him. This gentle encouragement eventually leads to what Mrs. Dashwood wants: a good match for Marianne. Love, generally speaking, doesn't enter into the equation for most parents. Mrs. Ferrars wants Edward to marry Miss Morton because she is wealthy and a *Lord*'s daughter even though he loves Elinor. She only wants him to marry at or above his social station, not below it and certainly not to a poor woman.

Characters

Elinor Dashwood

Elinor is the oldest of the three Dashwood daughters, and also the most reserved. She is affectionate, but she keeps her feelings in check when in public, unlike her sister Marianne. She is fiercely loyal to her sisters and looks after Marianne. She tends to put others before herself but sometimes tries to use them as excuses for not doing certain things: for example, when Elinor does not want to go to London in case she bumps into Edward, she uses their mother's health as the excuse instead of admitting the real reason why she does not want to go.

Marianne Dashwood

Marianne is the second oldest Dashwood daughter. She is talented, enthusiastic about the things she loves, and vocal about the things she does not like. Marianne is most like her mother, and they tend to wind each other up about things that make them emotional. She is obsessed with romance and the romantic ideal and has some naive ideas about love at the beginning of the novel. She can be seen as a kind of stereotype of the romance novel in that she overreacts, is prone to hysterics and fell for the man who literally swept her off her feet. Marianne comes to learn that her ideals have led her to fall in love with the wrong person, but she succeeds in the end by marrying Colonel Brandon.

Edward Ferrars

Edward Ferrars is Fanny Dashwood's brother, and John Dashwood's half brother. He first visits the family at Norland Park where he and Elinor end up close enough for the Dashwood family to expect them to marry. Edward's inconsistent behaviour throughout the novel is a source of mystery for Elinor, who first believes she has lost him because he is not in love with her, and then discovers he has been hiding a secret engagement for four years. Edward is loyal and honourable enough to stand by Lucy when he does not love her anymore.

Mr. John Willoughby

Willoughby is a man driven by his own pleasure. He rescues Marianne after she sprains her ankle and is immediately interested in her. They share their love of music and literature. He is outgoing and often speaks his mind when honour dictates he shouldn't have. For example, he insults Colonel Brandon for seeming old. Even though he does this when the Colonel is not within earshot, Willoughby's treatment of Brandon in front of the Dashwoods is unfair, particularly as this has stemmed from his guilty past. Willoughby abandoned a pregnant 15 year old after seducing her. After Mrs. Smith, the woman who controls Willoughby's inheritance, suggests he needs to marry the girl and he refuses, he finds himself in danger of losing his fortune. Willoughby is selfish enough to abandon Marianne without properly explaining himself and going after Miss Grey, a woman with a large enough fortune to satisfy his expenses. Although Willoughby returns later on to explain himself and beg for forgiveness—suggesting he actually has a conscience—many readers find the late apology strange, especially when Elinor and Marianne pity him for his loveless marriage.

Colonel Brandon

Colonel Brandon is a retired officer and one of Sir John Middleton's friends. He is a slightly older suitor at the age of thirty-five, which Marianne announces is far too old, and is generally a sensible, calm and thoughtful man. He looks after those in his care, including Eliza, and makes sure that the Dashwoods are protected. The journey he takes to retrieve Mrs. Dashwood for Marianne and his offer of a profession to Edward are clear pieces of evidence of his honourable nature. He suffered a loss of a loved one when the woman he loved was abandoned by his own brother, and this has given him considerable pain over the years.

Mrs. Dashwood

Mrs. Dashwood is the second wife to Henry Dashwood and gave him three daughters. She is most like Marianne, her middle daughter, in that they both grow hysterical and emotional over events that happen to them. They also share their romantic ideals. This tends to lead her to make poor decisions: for example, even though neither Marianne or Willoughby formally announced their engagement, she assumes that they are engaged because of the way they act around one another. Elinor suggests she should ask Marianne if they are engaged or not so that she can advise Marianne to be careful if they are not, but Mrs. Dashwood refuses to do so. She loves her daughters terribly and wants the best for them.

Sir John Middleton

Sir John Middleton is a distant relative of the Dashwood family and is quite a jolly but impolite man. His behaviour is often seen as vulgar, especially by Elinor who dislikes the way he teases her and others, including Colonel Brandon. Despite his vulgarity, he is a kind and generally loyal man who invites the Dashwoods to stay in the cottage on his grounds to rescue them from their difficult situation. He loves to throw parties and dinners for younger people and is an endless gossip alongside Mrs. Jennings, particularly where young couples are concerned.

Mrs. Jennings

Mrs. Jennings is Lady Middleton and Charlotte Palmers' mother. She has been widowed and has managed to marry off her daughters successfully, which means she is in constant need for distraction. She finds this in the Dashwood daughters, who she is determined to help marry off. She and Sir John love to gossip, but Mrs.

Jennings does have her more serious moments. When she can see someone has been deeply hurt, for instance when she discovers that Willoughby has abandoned Marianne, she is more concerned for Marianne than anything else.

Lucy Steele

Lucy Steele is the younger of the Steele sisters and generally considered a kind, sweet girl, but is decidedly more conniving and manipulative than she seems. She has been secretly engaged to Edward for the past four years and makes sure she forms close friendships with those who might be able to help her socially advance. When Robert Ferrars is named the new heir to the Ferrars fortune, Lucy all but jumps ship and decides she would rather marry him than Edward. She forms a close friendship with Elinor and confides in her about her secret engagement. While Elinor suspects this was out of paranoia that Edward had fallen in love with Elinor, there was no real evidence to support this suspicion.

Miss Anne Steele

Anne Steele, or Miss Steele, is the oldest of the two Steele sisters and is generally a vulgar, outspoken young woman without any real intelligence. She consistently reveals things in public that should not be spoken about, such as when she discusses the Doctor she quite fancies. Anne also tells Mrs. Ferrars about the secret engagement when she mistakenly believes that they are too well liked for the engagement to be opposed.

John Dashwood

John Dashwood is the son of Henry Dashwood from his first marriage, and the heir of the Dashwood fortune. He and his wife, Fanny, move into Norland Park and effectively make the rest of the Dashwood family homeless. John would be far kinder and loyal to the rest of his family if Fanny did not have her claws in him. He consistently suggests looking out for various members of the Dashwood family, particularly at the beginning when he is asked by his father to make sure they are protected. He also suggests that they could invite Marianne and Elinor to their home in London but is once again manipulated into coming to a different conclusion. He claims to be worried about his finances even though he and Fanny are rich, and this is generally because he has ambitions to be richer and to protect his money from the Dashwood family.

Robert Ferrars

Robert Ferrars is Edward's younger brother and well loved by their mother. He is the favourite son and is vocal about Edward's faults. He believes Edward should have been educated in public school, like Robert was, so that he was better prepared for life. After visiting Lucy repeatedly, Robert steals her away from Edward, suggesting he has little loyalty or love for his own brother. Robert is extremely vain and conceited, has a deep love for money and is proud of his manipulative exploits.

Mrs. Charlotte Palmer

Charlotte Palmer is one of Mrs. Jennings' daughters. She is a foolish, talkative woman, who loves to delight in anything she sees. Despite her own enthusiasm for everything she sees, her husband is completely the opposite. Charlotte thinks her husband is hilarious because of the way she acts, but it could be assumed that she is actually trying to avoid the pain she feels when he treats her that way.

Fanny Dashwood

Fanny Dashwood is John's wife, and Edward Ferrars sister. She is extremely vain and manipulative, much like her other brother, Robert. When John suggests something she does not approve of, she slowly pressures and persuades him to agree with her own, unvoiced decision. Just like her brother, Robert, and her mother, Mrs. Ferrars, Fanny is snobbish and looks at those below her as annoyances unless they serve a purpose to her at the time.

Lady Middleton

Lady Middleton is another one of Mrs. Jennings' daughters. She is withdrawn, reserved and generally only cares about her children. Her conversations mostly concern general knowledge, like the weather, and is a gentle lady. Elinor likes her because of her reserved nature, but Marianne thinks she is quite a dull woman.

Chapter Summaries

Chapter One

The Dashwood family had lived in Norland Park, Sussex for a long time. Everyone thought well of them because they lived in a fairly respectable house. The man who owned this house and estate had been single for a good while and had been living with his sister. She died ten years before, and he invited his nephew's family into the house. His nephew, Mr. Henry Dashwood, was the legal heir to Norland Park. He also had a number of children. In a former marriage, Mr. Henry Dashwood had had a son, and he also had three daughters by his current marriage. His son had a large fortune handed to him by his mother, and received even more when he married. Therefore, the inheritance of Norland Park would not mean much to a him—a man of fortune—and would be much more important to the three daughters. They had no fortune of their own, and their mother had nothing. Henry Dashwood's fortune was small because all of his first wife's money went to her son.

The old gentleman who owned Norland Park died. He left his estate to John Dashwood, Henry's son, and to John's own son, who had charmed the dead gentleman with his youth, and his earnest desire to have his own way. He did leave the three daughters with a thousand pounds each, however, to show his kindness. Henry had no way to protect or provide for his family, but tried to keep happy. He figured he would life for many years off the produce of Norland Park, but he died twelve months later leaving only ten thousand pounds to his widow and daughters. Just before Henry died, John was sent for. Henry begged him to take care of his mother-in-law and sisters. John agreed to do so, taken in by the emotions of the moment. Henry was at ease, and John had time to consider what he might do for them.

John was not a bad man—he was well respected, but a little cold hearted and selfish. It is suggested that had his wife, Mrs. John Dashwood, been a little kinder, he might have been even more respectable. As it stood, Mrs. John Dashwood was narrow minded and selfish. John first considered that he might increase the sisters' fortunes a little—he thought the extra four thousand a year, especially considering the fortune he already had and his own income made it a generous offer. He could spare the money without doing himself any wrong. However, straight after his father's funeral, Mrs. John Dashwood arrived with her son and their servants. No one could disagree with her visit as the house was John's straight after his father's death, but it was considered insensitive. Mrs. Dashwood, still mourning the loss of her husband, felt this insensitivity keenly and despised her daughter-in-law for it. She wanted to leave the house immediately, and for forever, but her eldest daughter, Elinor, encouraged her to think before she acted. Mrs. Dashwood decided to stay to avoid a rift in the family.

Elinor had a gift for understanding and an excellent judgement. Even though she was only nineteen years old, she was an excellent counsellor to her mother and frequently advised against behaviour which might be considered rude. She had enormous love and affection, but knew how to control them. Mrs. Dashwood had not learned how to do this, and neither one of Elinor's sisters could control their emotions, as a result. Marianne, the second eldest, was sensible and clever but too eager. Her feelings were expressed too acutely, and she reminded Elinor of their mother. Although Elinor saw the danger of wallowing in feelings, Mrs. Dashwood encouraged Marianne to do so. They gave into their sadness, encouraged it to continue and sought out new things that might make them sad. Elinor was upset, too, but had to greet her brother and sister-in-law with the attention they deserved and try to encourage the rest of the family to do the same.

Margaret was the third and youngest sister, and was fairly good humoured. However, she had already inherited too much of Marianne's dramatic sensibilities.

Chapter Two

Mrs. John Dashwood now considered herself the mistress of Norland. She downgraded Mrs. Dashwood and the sisters to mere visitors. They were, however, treated with civil respect by her, and with as much kindness as John could show to someone who was not himself, his wife or his child. He told them to consider Norland as their home, and as Mrs. Dashwood did not know where else they would go, the invitation was accepted. Mrs. Dashwood veered from exceedingly happy, to very sad. She took pleasure in both emotions.

Mrs. John Dashwood did not approve of her husband's plan to give the sisters three thousand pounds. It would turn their own son into a poor man! John did not have an argument against the accusation that he was stealing from his own son, especially when the Miss Dashwoods were only half related by blood. Mrs. John Dashwood considered that this was no relationship at all, and certainly not one that required such a large sum of money. John told her that his father had asked him to do it and that no sum in specific had been agreed on. He had only been asked to provide for them. Mrs. John Dashwood suggested that the sum should be less then, especially as they would never see that money again, and especially as their son might regret such a large sum of money being given away. Eventually, John came to the conclusion that 500 pounds would be a better sum of money. His wife agreed—the Dashwood sisters could not expect anything more from them, especially if they cannot afford it.

John then considered he might give Mrs. Dashwood 100 pounds a year to make their living easier. His wife hesitated and reminded John that Mrs. Dashwood might live for fifteen years and end up taking 1500 pounds from them. John doesn't believe she would live for that long, but his wife reminds him that people who are generally quite healthy and have money coming in live longer. It would also mean a yearly restriction on what John and she could spend. John agreed: if they would have to hand over money on a regular occurrence like it was rent, it would mean for a less independent life. His wife went on to suggest that those who rely on them for money would not show any gratitude for it because it would be expected. She suggests John should only give Mrs. Dashwood money when he wants to, so it appears more like a present. He agreed and will only give Mrs. Dashwood the occasional present of 50 pounds which will keep his promise to his father. Mrs. John Dashwood isn't convinced that his father meant for John to give them money at all—the assistance he spoke of might have actually referred to finding a home for them and sending them occasional presents. She then reminds her husband that the interest raised by the Miss Dashwood's small fortune would more than pay their mother this amount. She does not know what the family would even do with so much money—they won't keep horses, carriages, have company, hardly any servants and want for nothing. It is silly for them to be giving the family more money when they will barely spend the money they have already. John believed he finally understood his father's request: he will only provide Mrs. Dashwood with help when he wants to give her presents, and may even provide her with a present of furniture. Mrs. John Dashwood reminds her husband that when Mrs. Dashwood and Mr. Dashwood moved to Norland, they sold all the furniture and kept the linen and china. These have been left to Mrs. Dashwood in the will, and are of great quality, so why should they provide her with furniture too? They see it as evidence that Mr. Dashwood only thought of Mrs. Dashwood when he wrote the will, and if he could have, he would have left her with everything. John could not argue against such sound reasoning, and was resolved not to provide the family with anything more.

Chapter Three

Mrs. Dashwood and her daughters stayed at Norland Park for several more months, until Mrs. Dashwood grew tired of increasing her sorrow and was impatient to leave. She looked for a home in Norland, because she did not want to leave the area, but did not hear of anything that fit their budget or comfort. Elinor rejected the larger houses her mother might have approved so they did not overreach. Mrs. Dashwood had been told about her late husband's plea to his son, John, to protect the family, and she regretted treating John badly before, believing him to be a selfish man. Her contempt for Mrs. John Dashwood, however, grew. Living with them for half a year only increased her dislike of the woman. Neither woman would have been able to cope with the other had something not happened to warrant her daughters staying on at Norland.

Edward Ferrars, Mrs. John Dashwood's brother, was a pleasant gentleman who arrived at Norland Park to see his sister, and spent most of his time there. He and Elinor struck up an attachment and spent a lot of time together. Most mothers would have encouraged the match because Edward was rich, but Mrs. Dashwood was just pleased that they seemed to love each other. She did not believe in fortunes and inferior statuses breaking apart a pair of lovers, nor did she think anyone could ever reject Elinor.

Edward was not a handsome man, and his manners required getting to know him a little more to understand and approve of them. Once he overcame his shyness, his behaviour generally suggested an affectionate heart. His education was good, but his lack of distinct abilities or attitude towards what he wanted to do in life had led his mother and sister to despair. They wanted to see him established. His mother wanted him to get into politics and work alongside great men. Edward just wanted a quiet life. It was fortunate that the family had a more ambitious younger brother.

Edward had been staying in the house for several weeks before Mrs. Dashwood began paying attention to him. At the time, she had been thick in her depression and had been unable to see what was going on around her. She liked that he was quiet and did not disturb her thoughts. Elinor made a comment one day that compared him to his sister, Mrs. John Dashwood, which aroused her thoughts on him. That he was wholly unlike his sister more than recommended him to Mrs. Dashwood. She liked him already. Elinor suggested she would like him even more when she got to know him a bit better. After this, she endeavoured to do just that. She overcame his shyness and quickly uncovered his merits. That she believed he was in love with Elinor helped her in her estimation of him, but she was sure that he was a worthy gentleman. Mrs. Dashwood was certain that they would be married. She suggested to Marianne one day that Elinor would be settled in marriage soon. Marianne does not know what they will do without her, but Mrs. Dashwood insists they will not be separated by a large distance, and she will have gained an affectionate brother in Edward.

Marianne is a little surprised by Elinor's choice. She finds there is something wanting in him—that he lacks the spirit and fire which suggests virtue and intelligence, and that he has no taste for music or art at all. Marianne declared she could never be happy with someone whose taste differed so greatly from her own. When Edward read to them last night, she could not stand his tame recitation, and felt sorry for Elinor, even though she seemed not to care at all. Marianne believes Elinor does not share her intensity of feelings, and this is why she can be happy with him, but it would have broken her own heart had she had to listen to a man she loved read with such indifference. Marianne does not believe she will ever find someone worthy of her love, but Mrs. Dashwood tells her not to worry so much. She is only seventeen, and she will be as fortunate as her own mother was!

Chapter Four

Marianne declares that it is a pity Edward has no taste for drawing. Elinor thinks he does: even if he does not draw himself, he finds great pleasure in watching others do so. He has natural talents of his own, but has not had the chance to improve upon them; she thinks if he had, he would have drawn well. His self doubt means he is often unwilling to provide his opinions on a drawing, but has a generally sound understanding. Marianne was afraid of offending her sister, and so said no more. She considered her sister's feelings for Edward had made her blind to his true talents. Elinor suggests Marianne could not think Edward has poor taste in general, or she would never manage to be civil to him. Marianne asks her not to be offended if they do not share the same beliefs in Edward's merits and insists she has a high opinion of him. Elinor was pleased by this—she couldn't ask for anything more.

She goes onto talk about Edward's merits: that he has excellent understanding and principles, even though these are sometimes hidden behind his shy nature. While Marianne has been in conversation with their mother, Elinor has had many discussions with Edward on literature and his own taste. This has led her to believe Edward's mind is well informed, his imagination is lively, he enjoys books, and his observation and taste are well formed. Elinor also thinks he is quite handsome. Marianne will consider him handsome, too, if Elinor tells her to think of him like a brother. Elinor was startled by this: she did not think that there was so much certainty in their possible match, and tried to explain this to her sister. After admitting she "esteems" Edward, Marianne called her cold hearted and laughed at her. Elinor insisted that her feelings were much stronger than she could state and that she hopes he feels the same way. Beyond this, there was nothing else to announce. There are moments when even she doubts the extent of his feelings for her, and until she knows his feelings for certain, Marianne and Mrs. Dashwood must stop their conjecturing. Elinor also reminds Marianne that Edward's mother does not appear to be a woman who would so easily accept her son's marriage to a woman with neither a good fortune or rank. Marianne was astonished that she and her mother had failed to see the truth. Marianne is astonished to find they are not engaged, but is convinced it will happen soon.

Elinor believed Edward's occasional apathy might be due to the knowledge that his mother would not approve of the match. It meant Elinor could not feel at ease with her or his feelings. The more time they spent together, the more convinced she was that he did not wholly return her feelings and sometimes only considered her as a friend. Edward's sister perceived the feelings both Edward and Elinor might have for one another and took action. She talked to Mrs. Dashwood about her mother's plans to marry both of her brothers off well, and that a young woman attempting to draw him in would be in danger. Mrs. Dashwood could not pretend to not know what she was referring to, left the room and decided Elinor should not be exposed to further insult.

Thankfully, they received a letter offering a small house belonging to one of Mrs. Dashwood's relations. It was owned by a gentleman of fortune and property in Devonshire, and he assured Mrs. Dashwood in the letter that everything she wanted done to the cottage would be completed. He asked her to come to Barton Park to see Barton Cottage herself, but Mrs. Dashwood did not need anymore time to consider. Although it meant moving further away than she originally would have wanted, it meant that Elinor would no longer be in danger and that they would escape Mrs. John Dashwood. Mrs Dashwood wrote back to Sir John Middleton immediately and accepted his proposal. Elinor believed it was a good idea to move to a home away from Mr. and Mrs. John Dashwood, and liked the idea of a small cottage as it would be easy to keep. However she felt about Edward, she did not prevent her mother from sending the letter of acceptance.

Chapter Five

As soon as the letter was sent, Mrs. Dashwood announced to her son-in-law and wife that she had a house and would no longer be in their way as soon as they could leave. Mrs. John Dashwood said nothing. John hoped they would be close to Norland. Mrs. Dashwood had the greatest pleasure to announce they were going to Devonshire. Edward turned to Mrs. Dashwood, plainly upset that Elinor would be going so far away. She explained that the cottage was to their liking and that they could add a few bedrooms if required. She concluded the conversation with an invitation to Mr. and Mrs. John Dashwood, and an even nicer one to Edward so that they might visit in the future. Even though Mrs. Dashwood wanted to separate Elinor and Mrs. John Dashwood, she wanted to make it plain to them all that Edward would be welcome—she wanted to ensure that *their* relationship continued as she hoped. John was upset that he would not be able to assist in the move of the furniture, and everything was sent via water. Mrs. John Dashwood was not at all pleased that linen, china, books and a pianoforte so lovely was on its way to a home with limited income.

They sold the carriage, having sold the horses after Henry's death, and sent away most of their servants. Mrs. Dashwood hoped that John would make good on his promise to help them, especially now that they were leaving Norland, but grew steadily doubtful that he would do so. John started to complain at length about his dwindling fortune and the demands on him until it became clear that he would rather keep the money for himself, rather than give it away to others.

In a few weeks from the first letter of acceptance, everything was ready for their departure for Barton Cottage. On the last night, Marianne walked around Norland, crying, and despairing. She did not know when she would ever feel at home again, or if anyone would enjoy the grounds as much as she had enjoyed them.

Chapter Six

The first part of their journey was a sad one, but as they grew closer to their new home, their interest in their new environment overcame their sorrows. When they entered Barton Valley, they were happy with what they found. It was a lovely area of countryside, full of trees and farmland. At the cottage, a small green field lay, and a wicket gate lay in front of it. Barton Cottage was small and comfortable, but a defective cottage. The roof was tiled, the window shutters were not painted green, and the walls were not covered in honeysuckle. It was poor and small in comparison to Norland, but the arrival of the servants made them happier, as did needing to make each other happy and comfortable. There were some pleasant views of Barton village from the cottage, and their new home was surrounded by rolling hills. Mrs. Dashwood was pleased with the house and the furniture and would do them well for the present. They could not perform any repairs or additions until the next year, but Mrs. Dashwood hoped by then they'd have money to consider building additional rooms. They spent the rest of that night making the home theirs: they spread their belongings around, Elinor's drawings went up on the wall and Marianne's pianoforte was unpacked.

Just after breakfast the following day, Sir John Middleton arrived to check on them. He was a pleasant looking man of around forty years old, and had visited the family before, but the Miss Dashwoods were too young to remember him. He was friendly and good humoured. He urged them to have dinner at Barton Park every night until they were settled in their new home. Within half an hour after he left, a large basket of garden and fruit items arrived from Barton Park. By the end of the day, meat arrived at the cottage, too. He also insisted on taking their letters to and from the post for them, and would send them his newspaper every day. Lady Middleton sent a civil message with an invitation to wait on Mrs. Dashwood as soon as it would be convenient. Lady Middleton was a tall, striking woman of no more than 26 or 27 years old. She had elegant manners but lacked some of her husband's warmth. She had little to say beyond general remarks or questions. However, she did not need to talk. Sir John talked enough for both of them, and Lady Middleton had brought along her six year old son which took up much of the Miss Dashwood's conversation. Sir John secured their promise of dining at Barton Park the next day before he left them alone.

Chapter Seven

Barton Park was approximately half a mile from the cottage, and none of the Dashwoods had seen it yet, even though they had passed quite close to it. The house was large, handsome and elegant. They kept company and friends all the time—to the point where they had more company than any other family in the neighbourhood. This was extremely necessary to their happiness, because aside from hunting and being a mother, neither had anything else to do. Lady Middleton loved to be complimented on the domestic attributes of her home, and of the elegance of her dining table, while Sir John loved to surround himself with as any noisy, young people as his house would hold. The young people in the community loved him because he was always throwing parties during summer and private balls in winter.

The arrival of the Dashwoods brought Sir John great joy: the Miss Dashwoods were pretty girls, which immediately secured his good opinion of them. He took immense satisfaction in showing the Dashwoods kindness as it reflected his good heart. Sir John met them at the door of Barton Park and led them to the drawing room, returning to the same subject he had talked about the previous day: finding smart young men to meet them. He told them there would be another gentleman present, but he was not young or particularly carefree. He had hoped for more people to be present, but other families already had plans for that day. However, Lady Middleton's mother had arrived in the last hour, and she was a cheerful woman to talk to. He hoped the ladies would not find the gathering too dull or boring. The Dashwoods were perfectly happy.

Mrs. Jennings, Lady Middleton's mother, was a merry, fat old woman who talked a lot. She was happy and a little vulgar, full of jokes. Before dinner had even finished, she had commented on many subjects to do with lovers and husbands and hoped the Miss Dashwoods had not left their hearts behind in Sussex. Marianne was worried for Elinor's sake, and watched her to see how she bear these attacks. It was Marianne's look that gave Elinor more pain that Mrs. Jennings' general comments.

Colonel Brandon, Sir Johns friend, was silent and grave. He was not unpleasant looking, but he was older than 53. He had sensible, gentlemanly manners. There was nothing in any of these people which could recommend them as friends to the Dashwoods, but because Lady Middleton's countenance was so cold, even Colonel Brandon's serious nature was intriguing to them.

When they discovered that Marianne was musical, she was invited to play the pianoforte. Marianne sang well, playing through the sheet music Lady Middleton had brought with her from her former home before she was married. Marianne considered that the sheet music had probably not moved since it was first brought into the home. Marianne's performance was celebrated by all except Colonel Brandon, who, instead of loudly proclaiming his love for her playing, paid close and quiet attention to her.

Chapter Eight

Mrs. Jennings' two daughters had already been respectfully married, and, therefore, had nothing left to do with her time but marry off other people. She was active in this endeavour, and was quick to discover attachments between young people. She also liked to make ladies blush when she suggested they had power over certain men. This kind of investigation led her to announce that Colonel Brandon was in love with Marianne. She had suspected it when she saw how intently he listened to her play the piano, and she was convinced when they visited the cottage and saw the same behaviour from the Colonel. Mrs. Jennings was overjoyed, because it would make for a fine match—she was pretty and he was rich. It also provided her with ample entertainment, because she would laugh at the Colonel at Barton Park, and laugh at Marianne at the cottage. Once Marianne realized who Mrs. Jennings referred to, she was upset that such an old man would be attached to her. Mrs. Dashwood, only five years older than the Colonel, did not want to think of him as ancient, and insisted Mrs. Jennings was not making fun of the Colonel because of his age. Marianne urged her mother to see the accusation was absurd because the Colonel could be her father, and had probably already grown out of the feelings love provided. Marianne called the Colonel infirm, then, and both Elinor and Mrs. Dashwood laughed at her, teasing her for assuming the Colonel was close to death just because he was a little older.

Marianne considered that a woman of twenty seven years old would be a better match, because it would be a marriage of convenience. There would be nothing wrong in that. Elinor objects to dooming Colonel Brandon and his future wife to sickness just because Colonel Brandon complained about slight rheumatism in his shoulders the previous day. Marianne points out he mentioned wearing a flannel waistcoat, which suggests clearly to her that there will be more aches and pains to deal with, and most that the old and weak are afflicted with. Elinor thinks she would have liked him better had he been in the thick of a violent fever. Elinor then left the room.

Marianne confided in her mother that she thought Edward must be sick. They had been in the cottage for a fortnight by then, and he had not visited them. Mrs. Dashwood had no idea he would come so quickly to the cottage, and assures her she does not feel nervous at all on the subject. She wonders if Elinor expects him—Marianne insists she must, although they have not discussed it. Mrs. Dashwood thinks she is mistaken: when they discussed repairs to a spare bedroom, Elinor did not want to hurry with them because they were not expecting visitors for a long time. Marianne does not know what this means! She remembers how cold their goodbyes to each other were, and that there was no distinction in Edward's goodbyes to her and Elinor. Marianne had tried to leave them alone a few times in the last morning together, and he followed her out of the room every time. And, Elinor did not cry as much when they left Norland and Edward. She wonders if Elinor is upset, and if she is, when she finds time to show it.

Chapter Nine

The Dashwoods were settled at Barton and were in great comfort. The grounds and the house were now familiar to them, and they now enjoyed the same activities they used to enjoy at Norland before their father died. Sir John called on them every day for the first two weeks, and was amazed that they were always busy doing something. They did not have many other visitors, despite Sir John's insistence that they spend time with others and his offers that they should take his carriage, and Mrs. Dashwood only wanted her daughters to be friends with those who lived close by. The only house they had come across, which had reminded them a little of Norland, belonged to an old, weak woman who rarely socialized and never left her home.

There were many walks the girls could go on. Marianne and Margaret went for a walk one day eager to get out while it wasn't raining. Marianne assured them all that it would not rain, even though it had for the last two, but Margaret was the only one willing to go with her. When they reached the bottom of the hill, the winds had picked up. Marianne announced they would walk for two hours, and they walked against the wind. They walked for around twenty minutes before the heavens opened, and they were soaked with rain. With no shelter but their own house nearby, they had to turn around. They ran down a steep hill toward their garden gate, but Marianne stepped awkwardly and fell. Margaret, unable to stop running, made it to the bottom of the hill. A gentleman carrying a gun, with two dogs with him, was passing up the hill and was quite near Marianne when she fell. He put his gun down, and went to help. He took her in his arms, and carried her down the hill, through their garden and straight into the house. Mrs Dashwood and Elinor stood in shock and admiration. The gentleman apologized for intruding in their house, and they noticed how handsome and graceful he was. Although Mrs. Dashwood would have been grateful to him even if he was old and ugly, the fact that he was young and elegant gave her more to think about. She asked him to sit down, but he refused on account of how dirty and wet he was. She asked for his name—it was Willoughby, and his home was Allenham. He hoped he might call on Marianne the next day, which Mrs. Dashwood encouraged. He then left.

Marianne had seen much less of him than everyone else because she couldn't bring herself to look at him. She had, however, seen enough of him to admire him as much as the rest of the family did. She thought of him like a hero from a story, especially because he carried her into the house without stopping to make sure he had permission to do so. Marianne's imagination and admiration were in high gear.

Sir John visited the next day after hearing about Marianne's accident. They asked him about Willoughby; Sir John was surprised he was in the area. He decided he would ask him to dinner later that week. Mrs. Dashwood asked if that meant Sir John knew him. Willoughby visits the area every year, is a good man, and a fantastic hunter. Marianne pushed for more details regarding his pursuits and talents. Sir John did not know him that well. Elinor wondered who he was, and if he has a house at Allenham. Sir John revealed he had no property of his own and was only visiting the old woman who lived at Allenham Court. He was related to her and would inherit her possessions. Sir John insisted he was a good match, especially as he has his own estate in Somersetshire. He suggested to Elinor that she should not leave him to Marianne, especially as Colonel Brandon would be jealous. Mrs. Dashwood stepped in, then, and insisted that neither of her daughters would attempt to catch him as this was not how they were brought up, no matter how rich they are. She is pleased he is respectful. Marianne is overjoyed to hear Willoughby once danced for hours on end before getting up early to ride his horse. It proves he has spirit and passion. Sir John concludes Marianne has fixed her eye on Willoughby, and will never look at Colonel Brandon again. Marianne dislikes Sir John's way of speaking, and she tells him so. Sir John just laughed at her, and insisted she will make her conquest of Willoughby, regardless of how he speaks about the matter. He is, however, quite upset for Brandon, who has fallen in love with Marianne.

Chapter Ten

Willoughby—or, "Marianne's preserver", as Margaret called him—arrived at the cottage early in the morning to ask after Marianne's injury. Mrs. Dashwood welcomed him into the house with kindness, especially after hearing Sir John's compliments. During this visit, Willoughby more than proves Sir John's impression of him was correct, and has an opportunity to form his own opinions about the Dashwoods. Elinor had a delicate complexion, and was pretty, but Marianne was prettier—beautiful, even. He noticed the spirit in her eyes, particularly after she recovered from the shame of remembering her fall the previous day. When Willoughby announced he loved music and dancing, the look Marianne gave him made him want to talk to her for the rest of his visit. Marianne did not shy away from speaking up when a topic she was interested in was raised. They quickly learned that they shared a love for dancing, music, and literature. They shared favourite books and talked about specific passages from them. Before Willoughby left, they found themselves talking like old friends do.

Once Willoughby left, Elinor teased Marianne for doing well for one morning. She had discovered Willoughby's opinion on every topic considered important, specific authors and how passionate he is about each. Elinor joked she did not know how long their friendship would last when they would run out of things to talk about. Marianne cried that she wasn't being fair—she sarcastically suggested she should have been cold and reserved instead of at ease and open. Mrs. Dashwood told her Elinor meant no harm in what she said, and Marianne calmed down.

Willoughby visited every day. He first gave his need to check in with Marianne as an excuse, but then became so at ease with the family that he did not need one. Although Marianne was confined to the house, she was at least entertained by Willoughby who was affectionate and imaginative. They read, talked and sang together. He read with all the spirit and passion Edward had lacked. Mrs. Dashwood saw no faults in him. Elinor only thought he shared in Marianne's flaw of speaking their minds on every subject, regardless of how it might affect others. Elinor could not approve this lack of caution, particularly as it ignored general politeness in order to give into the desires of his heart. Marianne discovered, over time, that her doubt of finding a man to satisfy her expectations had been unjustified. Willoughby was everything she had imagined and hoped for. Mrs. Dashwood also hoped, by the end of that week, to expect Marianne and Willoughby married. She was secretly happy she would have Edward and Willoughy as sons-in-law.

Colonel Brandon's love for Marianne became obvious to Elinor, particularly now that others were too distracted by Willoughby to notice it. Although Elinor had assumed Mrs. Jennings had exaggerated the extent of Colonel Brandon's feelings for Marianne, she could now see Mrs. Jennings was absolutely right. She watched Brandon with a little concern—he had no chance against someone as young, rich and attractive as Willoughby. Elinor wished Brandon would drop his feelings for Marianne, particularly for his own sake, as Elinor did like him. He was still reserved, but Elinor believed this was because he suppressed his emotions, rather than due to any kind of temper. Sir John had dropped hints of past regrets and disappointments Brandon had suffered, and this justified Elinor's assumption. She felt sorry for him because Marianne and Willoughby liked to insult him for being old and reserved. Willoughby felt that Brandon was a man who everyone spoke well of and no one cared for. Marianne agreed, but Elinor disagreed—she spoke to him every time they were together. Willoughby only saw this as evidence that Elinor was nice to him, but no one else approved of him. Elinor argues that Brandon is a sensible man who knows a lot about the world, and is fairly intelligent. Willoughby and Marianne are not impressed by these arguments. Elinor wonders why Willoughby dislikes him so much, but he insists he does not dislike him—he respects him, but still provides three reasons why Colonel Brandon is not a favourite of his: he has threatened Willoughby with rain when he wanted it to be sunny, found fault with the hanging of his chariot, and could not persuade him to buy his brown mare. Willoughby is determined to dislike him as much as he wants.

Chapter Eleven

The Dashwood family had not imagined that they would have so many visitors and invitations when they moved to Devonshire. When Marianne was fully recovered, private balls at the Park, parties on the water and other amusements began. Willoughby was involved in every single one, and gave him the opportunity to get closer to the Dashwoods and for admiring Marianne. Elinor was not surprised at Marianne and Willoughby's attraction, but wished it was hidden a little better. She did suggest to Marianne to be a little more reserved, but Marianne hated to conceal her emotions and thoughts. She did not want to give way for mistaken feelings and thoughts, and as Willoughby felt the same way, they continued to openly show the way they felt. Everything Willoughby did was right to Marianne, and she had eyes for no one else when he was with her. If they danced, they danced together for half the night. If they had to stop dancing, because polite society demanded it, they would not dance with anyone else and stood close together. They were made fun of because of it, but this did not shame either of them. Mrs. Dashwood did not mind how open they were with their emotions because it was evidence of their youth and passion. Marianne's heart now belonged to Willoughby.

Elinor was not as happy, or at ease. She, unlike Marianne, still regretted leaving Norland. There was no one to supply her with conversation that rivalled that she had at Norland. Mrs. Jennings repeatedly told Elinor about her history, being someone who talked too much, and Lady Middleton was silent for much of the time. When she did speak, her feeling and conversation was the same as the day before.

In Colonel Brandon, however, Elinor found a person she could respect and become friends with. She did admire Willoughby, but his attention was entirely on Marianne, and he was too agreeable. Brandon found consolation in conversation with Elinor, especially when he found he had no encouragement to think of Marianne with hope. Elinor sympathized with him, particularly when she began to suspect he had been disappointed in love before now. This suspicion came out of a conversation they had one evening at Barton Park while the others were dancing. Brandon, looking at Marianne, suggested Marianne did not believe in second chances in love. Elinor replied that she was a romantic—she did not know how Marianne had come to this conclusion when her own father had been married twice, but she hoped her sister would settle down and become more reasonable with age. Colonel Brandon agreed, but thought there was something admirable in this kind of passion young people have. Elinor did not agree with this—Marianne constantly behaved impolitely, and Elinor hoped a little more understanding of the world might help her. After a moment, Brandon asked if Marianne was against all those who fell in love with a second person, even if they are disappointed by their first choice in a match. Elinor did not know the specifics of Marianne's thoughts, but had never heard her speak positively about a person making a second attachment. Brandon considered for a moment that Marianne might change her opinion, but then seemed to change his own mind. He feared that these youthful, passionate thoughts might give way for more dangerous ones. He begins to tell Elinor of a woman he knew like Marianne who ended up in trouble, but then stops himself when he realizes he has said too much. Elinor would not have thought much about this mentioned woman, but Brandon's hesitance to continue the conversation raised her suspicion. Whereas Marianne would have pushed the Colonel for the entire story, Elinor kept quiet and left Brandon to think about his past love.

Chapter Twelve

While Elinor and Marianne walked together the next morning, Marianne told Elinor that Willoughby ad given her a horse—one he had bred himself to specifically carry a woman. Marianne had not taken into consideration that her mother did not want to keep a horse—if Marianne kept it, she would need to keep a servant to ride it and have a stable to shelter it, and she had not stopped to ask permission before accepting the gift. Marianne wants to share the gift with Elinor so they could both ride it every day. Marianne was unwilling to listen to reason, even when Elinor suggested accepting a gift from a man she barely knew would be improper. Marianne brushes this off—she and Willoughby are as close as she is with Elinor and her mother. She believes that it takes some people years to get to know one another, and days for others. Elinor knew it was safer not to push the point further, especially given Marianne's temper. Later, Mrs. Dashwood told Marianne that the horse could not be kept, and Marianne agreed—however reluctantly—to decline the offer the next time she saw Willoughby.

She kept her promise, and the same day—when Willoughby visited—Elinor overheard Marianne explain she could not accept the present. Willoughby was concerned, but assured her the horse was still hers, that she could ride it when she wanted, and when she left Barton after marrying, the horse would belong to her. Elinor concluded, especially as Willoughby used Marianne's first name, that there was an agreement between them. She decided not to doubt their engagement from then on.

The next day, Margaret told Elinor she had watched Willoughby and Marianne together in the parlour. She was sure that they would be married soon, but Elinor reminded her she had been saying this since the first time they met. Margaret had even thought Marianne wore his picture around her neck, but it had been of their Uncle. Margaret insisted that she was right this time as Willoughby had a lock of her hair. He had cut it off after begging for it. He kissed it, wrapped it in a piece of paper and put it into his pocket book. Elinor could not deny Margaret her thoughts after this, especially as she thought the same way.

However, when Mrs. Jennings asked Margaret for the name of Elinor's favourite one night, Margaret turned to her sister and asked if she was allowed to tell. Elinor tried to laugh, but her heart was not in it. She was sure Margaret had thought of Edward, which in turn made Elinor think of Edward, and this hurt. She did not want Edward to turn into a standing joke with Mrs. Jennings. Marianne, feeling for her sister, turned to Margaret and told her off—she had no right to reveal her own conclusions. This only made Mrs. Jennings try harder to get the gentleman's name. She guessed that he lived at Norland, and was the curate at the parish, but Margaret denied this—he had no profession. Marianne, trying to gently persuade Margaret to not say anything, insisted Margaret had made this person up. Margaret reveals his name begins with an F. Marianne changed the subject quickly to the weather, and Elinor was grateful for it, even though Lady Middleton's dislike of these sorts of subjects would have led them into different subjects anyway. Regardless, Colonel Brandon took up the conversation of rain—always thoughtful enough to think of other's feelings—and they both talked for a while about the weather. The piano was then played, and the subject seemed to be dropped. Elinor, however, did not recover so easily.

Plans were made to visit somewhere twelve miles from Barton—a place that belonged to Colonel Brandon's brother-in-law. The grounds, said to be beautiful, had an area of water which could be sailed on, and they planned for a picnic. Although it seemed like a bold decision—it had, after all, rained every day for the last fortnight—it was generally agreed on. Mrs. Dashwood, at Elinor's request, would stay home out of the cold.

Chapter Thirteen

While Elinor had expected to be tired and soaked by the end of the visit, the trip ended up even more unfortunate because they did not even go. The entire group gathered at Barton Park to have breakfast. The weather appeared to be good, even though it had rained all night, and all were in decent moods. At breakfast, a series of letters were brought in. One was for Colonel Brandon, who, immediately turned pale when he saw it, and left the room. Sir John and the others wondered what was wrong. Lady Middleton assumed it could only be bad news if he left her breakfast table that quickly. When Colonel Brandon returned five minutes later, Mrs. Jennings pushed for details. Colonel Brandon refused to give any, and only told them it had come from town and regarded some business. Lady Middleton told Mrs. Jennings to think about what she was saying when she refused to accept Colonel Brandon's vague answer, but she ignored her. He denied it was from his cousin Fanny, and Mrs. Jennings revealed she knew who it was from, which made Colonel Brandon blush. He expressed his sorrow that he received the letter on this day because it regarded business which required him to return to town. Mrs. Jennings wondered what on earth he could need to do in town at this time of year, but Colonel Brandon continued on with his apologies—they would not be able to go to Whitwell because his own presence would be required. Marianne suggested writing a letter to the housekeeper, but Brandon did not think this would work. Sir John insisted Brandon would go to town the following day, but Brandon could not delay for an instant. Mrs. Jennings wanted to know what his business was so they could see if it could be delayed, or not. Elinor overheard Willoughby confide in Marianne that Brandon was probably worried about catching a cold and probably wrote the letter himself. Marianne agreed.

Lady Middleton assured Brandon that they would put off the event until Brandon returned. They all wanted to set a date, but Brandon could not—he did not know when he would be back next. Sir John promised he would come after Brandon himself if he did not return by the end of the week, and Mrs. Jennings agreed—at least he would be able to find out what Brandon's business was. Sir John replied that he did not pry into other men's business. Once Colonel Brandon's horse was announced, he said goodbye and then left. Once he had left the room, they all expressed their disappointment. Mrs. Jennings suggested she knew what Brandon's business was, and she is pressed for answers. She talks about Miss Williams, who is a close relation of Brandon's: his daughter.

Sir John returned to the room after seeing Colonel Brandon off, and announced they should do something together to be happy despite the disappointment. They call for the carriages so that they can go for a drive; Marianne gets into Willoughby's, and is pleased for it. The carriage is so fast that it is out of sight until they all return to Barton Park. Both seem delighted with the drive. They then decide to have a dance in the evening. At dinner, Mrs. Jennings told Marianne she knew where they had gone on their drive, and hoped that she liked her new house at Allenham. Marianne, now confused, turned away. Elinor discovered that Mrs. Jennings had looked into it because she had been so curious as to where they had gone. Elinor could not believe this to be true as Marianne could not have entered the house while Mrs. Smith still lived in it—they were not even acquaintances.

Once they left the dining room, Elinor asked her if it was true, and was surprised to find out it was. Marianne was angry with Elinor for doubting it—didn't Elinor want to see the house too? Elinor did but not while Mrs. Smith and no one else, but Willoughby was there. Marianne argued that Willoughby, being the heir, had every right to show her the house, and as they went in an open carriage, they physically could have no one else with them. Elinor does not think her actions were proper, even if the were enjoyable. Marianne argued she would not have enjoyed herself had her actions been improper—she would have felt that she was acting wrongly. Elinor then asked if Marianne had begun to doubt this evaluation of her behaviour, especially now that Mrs.

Jennings had suggested it was irregular, but Marianne does not. If Mrs. Jennings' remarks would guide their behaviour, they would always be doing something rude. Elinor tells her sister that even if she did become Willoughby's wife, her actions would not be justified. Marianne blushed, went away for a few minutes, and then returned to admit her behaviour might have been a little improper, but Willoughby had wanted to show her the house. Marianne went on to describe a sitting room in detail, and Elinor was sure she would have continued describing each room in detail had she not been interrupted by others.

Chapter Fourteen

Colonel Brandon's abrupt departure held Mrs. Jennings' curiosity for a few days. She was forever curious about her friends and acquaintance's actions; she was sure that Brandon had received some bad news, and listed in her mind every kind of distress that could have sent him fleeing into town. She considered it could be money problems, particularly as his estate did not appear to have a substantial income. She then thought about Miss Williams, and how self conscious Brandon had looked when her name was mentioned. Mrs. Jennings was convinced that Miss Williams was a sickly child, so this was a plausible reason, too. After a few more considerations, Mrs. Jennings wished he would be rid of all his troubles and find himself a wife. Elinor, despite her care for Brandon's welfare, did not share in Mrs. Jennings' never ending worries.

Elinor was more worried that neither Marianne or Willoughby had made public what seemed to have already been decided on. Their behaviour seemed to suggest that they had an understanding of marriage in the future, but nothing had come of it, and neither had spoken to Mrs. Dashwood. Elinor considered that it might be due to Willoughby's fairly low income which kept them from being public with their engagement, but it was strange to keep everything so secret. It was so strange that Elinor wondered if they were engaged at all. Willoughby showed his love to Marianne, and was considered almost a son and brother at Barton Cottage, which he loved like a second home and spent most of his hours there. A week after Colonel Brandon left in a hurry, Mrs. Dashwood mentioned that she would be improving the cottage. Willoughby opposed any kind of alteration. He did not want a single stone to be added. Elinor assured him there was not enough money to attempt it. Willoughby announced if he had the money, he would tear down his own house and rebuild a replica of the cottage in its place. Elinor wondered if he would include the cottage's faults, and teased him for thinking of their house as better than his estate. Willoughby insisted that there are reasons why he loved the cottage, but it was generally due to one specific reason. Mrs. Dashwood looked at Marianne then, both of them understanding Willoughby completely. Willoughby remembers when no one lived in Barton Cottage, and how he had little interest when he heard someone would be moving into it. He did not want the place he found happiness to be changed. Mrs. Dashwood assured him she would not change anything. Willoughby asked her to extend that promise even further and assure him they will always treat him with the same kindness. They promised him.

As Willoughby left, Mrs. Dashwood asked him to dinner the following evening and the invitation was accepted.

Chapter Fifteen

Mrs. Dashwood visited Lady Middleton the next day with Elinor and Margaret. Marianne excused herself from the visit, and Mrs. Dashwood assumed Willoughby had promised to call on her while the others were visiting Barton Park. When they returned to the cottage, they found Willoughby's carriage and servant waiting. Everything was as Mrs. Dashwood foresaw. However, when they stepped into the house, Marianne came running out of the parlour crying. They stepped into the parlour to find Willoughby leaning against the mantlepiece, not crying, but visibly upset. Mrs. Dashwood wondered if Marianne was ill. Willoughby tried to look cheerful, then, and hoped Marianne was well. He admitted he was disappointed because Mrs. Smith was sending him to London on business. He had to leave that morning. Mrs. Dashwood hoped that the business would not keep him away for long, but Willoughby admitted he did not have plans or any idea when he would return to Devonshire. He usually did not repeat his visits to Mrs. Smith more than once a year. Mrs. Dashwood insisted that others might invite him to their houses—she wondered if he could wait for an invitation to the cottage. He could not answer. She added that he would always be welcome at the cottage, but did not want to pressure him too much, knowing his engagements were wrapped up in Mrs. Smith's wishes. Willoughby could not speak for a moment, until he announced he would not torture himself by staying with friends he could not enjoy spending time with. Willoughby left.

Mrs. Dashwood could not speak and left the room. Elinor was anxious; Willoughby's embarrassment in leaving them, and his unwillingness to accept the invitation to the cottage was so unlike the behaviour of a lover that it disturbed her. She feared that either he had had no serious intentions to marry Marianne, or that there had been a large argument between them. The distress in which Marianne left the room seemed to suggest an argument even though her love for him meant an argument would be almost impossible. Mrs. Dashwood returned to the room within half an hour, but it was clear she had been crying. They discussed the sudden change in his behaviour from exceedingly happy to leaving with only ten minutes notice. He did not behave like himself and did not accept the invitation to the cottage. Mrs. Dashwood did not think he had the power to accept the invitation, and that everything makes sense to her now that she has thought this through. She believes Mrs. Smith suspects his love for Marianne and disapproves of it, perhaps because she has other plans for him and wants to get hm away from her. She has invented an excuse to send him away from Devonshire. She also believes that Willoughby knows Mrs. Smith disapproves and is obligated to leave. Elinor is not satisfied by this answer. Mrs. Dashwood accuses Elinor of being incapable of seeing Willoughby in a good light within this situation, and would rather blame him for it than believe he had no choice. Elinor defends her suspicion because of how changed his behaviour was toward them. It would have been more like Willoughby to admit to the reasons sending him away than hiding them. Mrs. Dashwood wonders if she's accusing them both of concealing things. Elinor does not need evidence of their affection for one another, but she does want evidence of their engagement. Mrs. Dashwood believes they are engaged, but Elinor points out that no words have been spoken on the subject. Mrs. Dashwood does not need words—it is clear to them all that Willoughby and Marianne love one another. She is surprised Elinor doubts their engagement when Willoughby's behaviour suggests otherwise; they are almost family, and it is impossible for him to have left Marianne without having confided in secret with her about their love. This is why she believes Marianne is so upset. Elinor will be satisfied if they do continue to speak despite Willoughby leaving. Mrs. Dashwood tells her daughter off—she does not require any proof, and wonders if Willoughby has ever given her reason to doubt his honour. Elinor loves Willoughby like a brother, and it is not easy for her to deal with her confusion. Even though Willoughby did not talk, or act like himself, Mrs. Dashwood's own reasoning may explain why. Mrs. Dashwood is satisfied by this answer. She believes secrecy may be the best option in this case, anyway.

Margaret interrupted them then by coming into the room, and Elinor could then think about her conversation with her mother. They did not see Marianne until dinner, where she did not say a word and looked as if she had been crying. She even avoided looking at them. When Mrs. Dashwood touched her hand with compassion, Marianne burst into tears and left the room. She had no control over herself, and the slightest mention of Willoughby sent her into a similar state.

Chapter Sixteen

Marianne could not have forgiven herself if she had been able to sleep the night Willoughby left. She was awake the entire night and cried for the majority. She got out of bed with a headache, didn't want to talk or eat, and refused all attempts at kindness from her family. When breakfast was finished, she walked out of the house by herself and wandered around Allenham village, indulging herself in remembering the past and crying. That evening she played every favourite song she used to play to Willoughby, and sat at the piano looking at the sheet music he had written out for her until she could not be any sadder than she was.

However, Marianne could not keep up her depression for too much longer. In a few days, she calmed down, but she still continued with her solitary walks and silent thinking. They received no letter from Willoughby, and Marianne did not seem to expect any. Elinor was uneasy, but Mrs. Dashwood found an explanation for that too. Sir John collects their mail, and to maintain secrecy he could not write to them. Elinor agreed that this was a possibility, but wanted to end their speculation by asking Marianne directly if she was engaged to Willoughby. If Mrs. Dashwood asked, it would not cause offence, particularly as they were open with each other. Mrs. Dashwood refused: if she asked, she might cause Marianne more pain if they are engaged—reminding her of Willoughby would upset her. She also refuses to force a confession for something which was obvious to them all. Elinor tried to make her see sense, but Mrs. Dashwood was convinced her daughter would tell her when she wanted to.

One night, Mrs Dashwood mentioned Willoughby's name. They had not finished reading Hamlet, and she suggested that they would save it for when he returned—even if it took him months. Marianne did not believe he would be gone for months—he would only be gone for a few weeks. Elinor was pleased with her response, because it meant that they had talked about the future and his plans.

One morning, Marianne joined her sisters on their usual walk rather than walking by herself. They came across a gentleman on horseback riding towards them. Marianne believed it was Willoughby who had returned to them, and to her. Elinor did not believe it was him, but Marianne was convinced. As they came closer, they saw it was Edward Ferrars. He walked back with them to Barton Cottage. They all welcomed him with kindness, but Marianne showed more warmth than any of them. Edward did not, Marianne observed, seem to treat Elinor with any more affection than the others. She was surprised. Marianne asked if he had come from London. Edward had been in Devonshire for a fortnight. She was surprised he had been in the county for so long without coming to visit Elinor. They asked about Norland, which prompted the family to remember it. Marianne mentioned the allure of the Autumn weather, but Elinor did not share her love of dead leaves. Marianne suggested that her feelings were not often shared, but were sometimes. At this, she seemed to think deeply, and shook it off. Edward asked if the Middleton family were good company. Marianne exclaimed they were not. Elinor told her off for saying that because they have had so many nice days together, but Marianne reminded them of the painful moments they had also experienced. Elinor ignored this and paid attention to Edward. His coldness made her angry, but she decided to treat him as he should be treated because of their family connection, and no more.

Chapter Seventeen

Mrs. Dashwood was not as surprised to see Edward because she had thought he would come to Barton Cottage. She gave him the kindest welcome out of all of the Dashwoods, and soon Edward became more like his old self. He was, however, not exactly like his old self, and all of the Dashwoods noticed it. Mrs. Dashwood decided this must be due to his mother, and asked after her and her pressures on him. Edward is still adamant he will not be made famous in any public arena as he has no ambition. He will be happy, but greatness and fame will not make him happy. Marianne agrees with him, but Elinor believes wealth has something to do with happiness. Marianne tells her off—it provides no real satisfaction—but Elinor points out it is required for material comfort. Marianne believes two thousand pounds a year as income is fairly moderate—no family could be maintained on any smaller. Edward is surprised by the list of items she believes a household needs. Margaret interrupts and wishes that someone would give each of them a fortune. They all join in imagining what each of them might do. Edward imagines they would buy books, sheet music and art work. Marianne would give money to the author who wrote that it would be impossible to be in love with more than one person in their life as her opinion on that point has not changed. Edward thinks she is a little more serious than she used to be, but Marianne thinks he is more serious than she is. He and Elinor discuss misinterpreting other people's personalities—he has thought of Marianne as a lively, energetic girl, when she is genuinely eager more than anything else. Elinor admits she has found herself making a few mistakes assuming what people's personalities are like. She can't even usually pinpoint how the mistake or deception was made—sometimes it is guided by what the person says about themselves, and usually by other people's opinions. Marianne thought it was right to be guided by the opinions of other people because their own judgements were inferior. Elinor only wanted to guide the behaviour of a person using other people's opinions, not to adopt their opinions for their own. Their conversation leads to Marianne's general behaviour. Edward wonders if she has not started to act properly, but Elinor admits she has. Edward admits he suffers from shyness, particularly around those who do not act properly. He believes he would be less shy if he could stop seeing himself as inferior. Marianne tells him he would still be reserved, which is even worse, to which Edward is surprised. Elinor laughs her comment off—she claims anyone who does not act like she does is accused of being "reserved". However, Edward did not answer her and sat for some time in thought and silence.

Chapter Eighteen

Elinor was upset that Edward seemed so unhappy. He was also confusing: one minute he acted as he did when they were close, and the next he became closed off and reserved. He joined Elinor and Marianne in the breakfast room the next morning, and Marianne left them alone in the hopes of encouraging them. Edward came out of the door after her and was surprised by it. He announced he was going into the village to check on his horses and would be back when breakfast was ready.

Edward returned later full of admiration for the countryside. This was a subject Marianne always wanted to talk about, and began to ask him for specific objects and views he had liked the most. Edward interrupted her by telling her not to ask too many questions because he did not have much knowledge about beautiful countrysides. Marianne admits that this is true, but wonders why he boasts that he does not have this knowledge. Elinor believes Edward sees other people pretending that they love nature more than they actually do or feel, and so he tries to pretend he does not have the ability to discriminate between different the beauty of several views. Marianne agrees that everyone has had to use the same sort of language to describe the countryside and detests it herself. Edward is convinced that Marianne feels precisely what she said she does, but begs her to allow him to feel no more for the countryside than what he has already stated.

Later on, as Edward took his tea cup from Mrs. Dashwood, Marianne saw he was wearing a ring with a lock of hair through it. She asked him if it was Fanny's hair, as she had not seen him wear a ring like that before. She wondered if it could be Fanny's hair even though it was a fantastic deal lighter than she would have thought. Edward blushed, and admitted it was his sister's hair. Elinor and Edward looked at each other then, and Marianne was sure that the hair was Elinor's, and not Fanny's. Edward was fairly embarrassed, and Marianne was upset that she had said anything.

They were visited by Sir John and Mrs. Jennings, who had heard that Edward had come to visit. They discovered Edward's surname began with "F" and mentally prepared comments they would use against Elinor when they were no longer within earshot of Edward. Sir John usually invited the Dashwoods back to Barton Park for tea or for dinner, but this time he asked them to come for both. Mrs. Jennings suggested that there would be a dance, particularly as many people were attending the dinner. Sir John wished that Willoughby was with them, which made Marianne blush, and Edward to grow suspicious. He asked Elinor who the gentleman was, and she gave him a brief reply. As time wore on, Edward considered for a few moments, and then went up to Marianne to suggest he knew what kind of relationship they had. Marianne hopes that he will like Willoughby when they meet, and Edward did not doubt he would.

Chapter Nineteen

Edward stayed at Barton Cottage for a week. Mrs. Dashwood asked him to stay longer, but he wanted to leave just when he was enjoying himself the most with his friends. He grew to love the house in his last few days and when he spoke of leaving never did so without sighing and regretting it. He did not have any demands on his schedule, and no idea where he would go, but he still had to leave them. He did not take pleasure or enjoyment in either Norland or London, but must return to either of them, even though he was happy at the cottage. Elinor explained Edward's behaviour away by referring to the demands of his mother on his schedule. She was happy that she did not actually know Edward's mother, because she could blame any unusual behaviour on her. Edward's lack of happiness and openness was explained away due to his need for and lack of independence, and the shortness of his visit due to needing to meet up with his mother again. Although Elinor would have loved to know when Edward's mother would end demands on her son so that he could be happy, she did not know if it would happen. She returned to her memories of their past days at Norland together for a bit of peace, and the ring around his finger with the lock of hair in it. Elinor was sure it was hers.

At their last breakfast together, Mrs. Dashwood told Edward he would be a happier man if he had a profession to fill his time up, especially as he would know where to go next when he left his friends and family's houses. Edward admits he has thought about this for a while. He has not been able to agree with his family on the choice of profession, however, particularly as Edward had always preferred the Church and his family did not think it was smart or great enough. They suggested the army or law, but neither of those interested him. As a result, he entered Oxford to study and has done nothing since. Mrs. Dashwood concluded that his own sons would be brought up with many pursuits to employ their time. Edward grew serious for a moment and suggested they would be brought up to be the opposite of him in every way. The others tell him to cheer up, and not to talk that way because he is suggesting that everyone opposite to him must be happy. Mrs. Dashwood tells him to find something that makes him happy, and in time his mother will accept whatever it is he has decided to do as it will prove his independence. Edward left soon after, and Elinor was determined not to give in to her uncomfortable feelings by keeping busy and doing everything the opposite to Marianne in the depths of her sadness. Without keeping herself away from her family, or awake at night, Elinor still found time to think about Edward and his behaviour.

One morning, company arrived while Elinor was sitting alone in the house. Sir John, Lady Middleton, Mrs. Jennings and two others—a gentleman and lady—had arrived. Sir John left the group to ask Elinor if she liked the strangers he had brought to the house. Although Elinor was mortified—fearing they might hear him talk—Sir John insisted that they weren't to be feared. These were the Palmers. He wondered where Marianne had gone to as her pianoforte was still open—he wondered if she had run away on seeing them coming. Marianne was out walking. Mrs. Jennings then joined them and spoke through window at them. It is revealed that the Palmers are her son and daughter. They arrived late last night. Mrs. Dashwood and Margaret came down the stairs, and the rest of the group entered the house Mrs. Palmer was years younger than Lady Middleton and unlike her in every aspect. She was short, plump, with a pretty face and good humoured manners, even though they were not as elegant as her sister's. She smiled a lot and laughed. Her husband was a serious looking man—he was less willing to be happy or make others happy than his wife. He bowed to the ladies, and then sat down to read a paper without saying a word. Mrs. Palmer, on the other hand, spoke at length. She complimented the parlour with enthusiasm and asked for her husband's opinion on the matter. Mr. Palmer did not respond. Mrs. Palmer joked that her husband often didn't hear her, and laughed. Mrs. Dashwood did not find this funny: she had never found ignoring someone humorous or witty. Mrs. Jennings continued to tell them the story of how the Palmers had arrived at Barton Park, and that she had hoped Mrs. Palmer would have stayed home that morning to rest, but her daughter wouldn't. When Mrs. Jennings suggested that Mrs. Palmer was pregnant and would be confined to her bed in February, Lady Middleton could not deal with the conversation anymore and asked Mr. Palmer if there was any news.

Sir John, seeing Marianne coming home, went to the front door to help her inside. Mrs. Jennings asked if she had been to Allenham, and Mrs. Palmer laughed so much that everyone was sure she knew what Mrs. Jennings actually meant by the question. When Lady Middleton stood to go, Mr. Palmer set aside his newspaper and stood. Mrs. Palmer joked that her husband had been asleep, but he made no answer. Sir John asked them to spend the following day at Barton Park: they attempted to excuse themselves on account of the weather being bad, but Sir John insisted that a carriage would come and pick them up. The rest of the group all asked them to come, too, and the Dashwood sisters had to agree to attending. After the group had left, Marianne commented that even though the rent of the cottage was low, they still had it on hard terms if they had to go to dinner with every single one of the Middleton's visitors. Elinor pointed out that their behaviour had not changed since they had arrived—it was probably their own feelings that had changed, and the parties which had made them happy before were now boring and tedious.

Chapter Twenty

As the Dashwood sisters entered the drawing room at Barton Park the next day, Mrs. Palmer came running in the other door, just as merry and happy as the day before. She is pleased to see them, especially as the weather is so bad; she didn't know if they would even come, which would be upsetting as they are leaving Barton Park the following day. She hoped that they would meet in London, but the Dashwood sisters insisted that they would not be going to London anytime soon. Mrs. Palmer would be disappointed if they didn't—she would be able to get the nicest house for them, right next to theirs, and would chaperone them at any time until she would have to be confined to their bed. They thanked her but resisted her pleas. When Mr. Palmer entered the room, his wife asked for his help persuading the girls to come to London, but he made no answer and instead began to complain about the weather. He hated being trapped inside because the rain made everything indoors more boring He was also upset that there was no billiards room in the house.

When the rest of the group had gathered together, Sir John mentioned that Marianne would not have had the opportunity to take her usual walk to Allenham. Marianne said nothing but looked serious and sad. Mrs. Palmer told her not to be so shy because they all know about her and Willoughby, and approve of her taste in men. Mrs. Palmer believed that they lived close to Willoughby, but Mr. Palmer assured her it was farther off than she thought. Mrs. Palmer had never been to his house, but most have told her it is a pretty place. Mr. Palmer thinks the house is vile. He continues to speak out against anything that his wife says, but Mrs. Palmer did not seem to be hurt by any of these instances. Elinor believed Mr. Palmer behaved in this way to appear superior to other people. She wondered why he did this, but considered it might be to prevent him from being attached in any way to people except for his wife.

Later, Mrs. Palmer asked Marianne and Elinor to come to Cleveland to visit them at Christmas, especially when the Westons are visiting. Mr. Palmer, after being pushed by his wife, sarcastically agreed he had no other reason to come to Devonshire but to invite the Dashwoods there. Both declined the invitation. Mrs. Palmer insisted they should come, especially as many people visited them these days. Mr Palmer was canvassing for an election to parliament and was forever bringing people to the house as visitors. Although it made him tired, especially when he had to try forcing others to like him, she thought it would be amusing to see MP next to his name.

Mrs. Palmer asked Elinor if she liked Mr. Palmer. Elinor said she did. Mrs. Palmer was glad, especially as he seemed pleased with the Dashwood family. She assured Elinor he would be disappointed if they did not visit Cleveland, and did not know why they refused to come. Elinor declined the invitation and changed the subject right away. She wondered if Mrs. Palmer could give her information about Willoughby, especially if they lived in the same county as one another. Mrs. Palmer had never spoken to him, but she saw him in town quite a lot. She knows why Elinor asks after him—Marianne is to marry Willoughby. Elinor is surprised that she seems so certain the marriage will happen! She tells Elinor not to deny it, especially as everyone is talking about it. She even met with Colonel Brandon before they left town, and he told her about it. Elinor thinks she must be mistaken: Colonel Brandon would not reveal or suggest information to those not directly involved. It was unlike him. Mrs. Palmer describes the meeting: when they walked together, they talked of her brother and sister, which led to the discussion about the Dashwoods. She mentioned that one of the Dashwood sisters would be married to Willoughby, and Colonel Brandon's reaction made it clear to Mrs. Palmer that this was true. She wondered when the wedding would be, but Elinor changed the subject by asking if Colonel Brandon was well. Mrs. Palmer assures her he is, and had nothing but compliments for the Dashwoods. Elinor pushed for more information about Willoughby, then, and she revealed not many people were friends with him because his house is far away, but those who know him like him. Marianne is lucky to ensnare him. Although Mrs. Palmer did not reveal a fantastic deal about Willoughby, any positive testimony about him was welcome. Elinor then asked if she had known Colonel Brandon for a long time. She had, and she was even almost married to him, but Mrs. Jennings wouldn't allow it. Elinor discovers he never actually told her he wanted to marry her, or even asked Mrs. Jennings, but Mrs. Palmer was sure that Sir John wished for the match, and had her mother not objected, Brandon would have been pleased with her.

Chapter Twenty-One

The Palmers returned to Cleveland the following day, leaving the Middleton and Dashwood families to entertain one another again. This, however, did not last long. Elinor was still wondering about Charlotte Palmer's never-ending happiness, and her strange relationship with her husband, before Sir John and Mrs. Jenning's brought more visitors to Barton. Mrs. Jennings had spent a morning in Exeter with Sir John and had met two ladies, who she discovered to be relations of hers. This was enough to justify Sir John inviting them back to Barton Park as soon as they were finished with their business in Exeter. Lady Middleton was nervous to have two strangers coming to her home, especially when they were relations of the family, too. Mrs. Jennings told her to keep calm—she would just have to put up with her cousins. As Lady Middleton was unable to prevent their visit, she gently told her husband off for it five or six times a day.

The young ladies arrived: they were dressed well, had civil manners, and were so fond of children that Lady Middleton thought well of them within an hour of their arrival. She thought they were lovely girls—a statement which, for her, was enthusiastic! Now that Sir John felt confident he had judged correctly in bringing the girls to Barton, he left to fetch the Dashwoods. He told them of the Miss Steele' arrival, and assured them that they were sweet girls. Elinor knew that there were sweet girls everywhere in England, so this was nothing exceptional. Sir John wanted them to walk to Barton immediately to see his guests. Lucy, one of the Miss Steele' sisters, is described by Sir John as a pretty and friendly girl. All of the children love and group around her like they're old friends, especially as the Steele sisters have brought toys for them. The Steele have heard in Exeter that the Dashwoods are beautiful ladies, and wanted to see them. Sir John insisted that they come, especially as they are probably related to the Dashwood family, too. However, the Dashwoods refused and only promised to visit the Park within a day or two. He walked home, amazed by their indifference.

As promised, the Dashwoods visited Barton Park to see the Steele sisters. They did not think the older sister, around thirty, was exceedingly pretty, but the youngest—no more than twenty-three years old—was uncommonly beautiful. Their manners were civil, and Elinor thought they were quite sensible, especially when she saw them making an effort with Lady Middleton. They spent much of their time complimenting and paying attention to the children, while the rest of their time was spent paying attention to what Lady Middleton was doing, or complimenting her on her dress. Lady Middleton, however, saw that the Steele sisters were allowing her children to do anything they wanted: they pulled the ladies' hair, untied their sashes, and stole their things. The youngest child, Annamaria, is scratched by a stray pin on one of the Steele sisters' dresses, and starts to scream. While Lady Middleton was alarmed, the Steele sisters outdid her in every way. They rushed to her aid: Lady Middleton sat the child on her lap and kissed her, the wound was bathed, and she was given sweets. The child did not stop crying, so she was taken out of the room by Lady Middleton. The two boys followed, leaving the Steele and Dashwood sisters alone together.

Miss Steele, the eldest, thought it might have been a terrible accident. Marianne did not know how it could be, unless it took place under entirely different circumstances. Lucy Steele complimented Lady Middleton on her sweetness, but Marianne could not reply. It was generally impossible for Marianne to not say what she genuinely thought, so Elinor had to tell a series of polite lies. Elinor, after each of the Steele' compliments, replied in kind, but without as much enthusiasm. The discussion of the Middleton children has them at odds: the Dashwoods prefer children who are better behaved, while the Steele cannot bear children who have been tamed.

After a short period of silence, Miss Steele asked the Dashwoods if they missed Sussex. The question itself seemed to suggest that they knew each other better than they did, which surprised Elinor. Miss Steele asked if Norland was beautiful, and Lucy added that Sir John had described it them as a kind of apology for her older sister's questioning. Miss Steele suggested that they did not have many handsome men at Barton as they did at Norland, and wondered what they did with their time. Lucy, ashamed of her sister, was amazed she had suggested that there were no handsome men in Devonshire. Miss Steele didn't mean to suggest that, but she did not know if there were more at Norland than at Barton. She asks if John Dashwood was good looking before he was married. Elinor did not quite understand what she meant, but assures her if he was before he was married, he still was. Miss Steele disagreed: no one should think of married men as handsome "beauxs" as they have another job to do now. Lucy asked her sister to stop talking about "beauxs" or the Dashwoods would assume she thought about nothing else. Lucy changed the subject quickly. Elinor thought Miss Steele was vulgar and silly, which she did not appreciate. She was also not impressed by Lucy's beauty, and so she left the house not wanting to know either girl any better. The Steele sisters felt the opposite: they declared that the Dashwoods were the most beautiful, elegant and accomplished girls they had ever come across and wanted to get to know them better. As Sir John agreed with this, Elinor found she had little chance to object and had to sit with them for an hour or two every single day. Sir John, believing that to get to know someone better meant simply sitting with them, believed that they would be friends soon. He did, however, tell both the Steele sisters everything which he knew, or suspected, the Dashwood sisters had encountered since they had come to Barton. They had not sat together more than two times before Miss Steele congratulated them on Marianne's conquest of Willoughby. She hoped Elinor would be able to find someone for herself, too, and then suggested she might already have someone in mind. Elinor knew that Sir John would have told them about her love for Edward, especially as he had already told them about Willoughby. In fact, at dinner it became a constant joke to remind Elinor of the man who had an "F" in his name, which raised Miss Steele' curiosity to know exactly who they were referring to. Sir John revealed Edward's name to her. Miss Steele congratulated Elinor on capturing Edward—she claimed to know him terribly well herself. Lucy told her off as they did not know him very well at all. They had seen him once or twice at their Uncle's house but knew no more about him than that. Elinor wanted the conversation to continue so that she could know more about this Uncle, but nothing else was said. For the first time since she came to Barton, she thought Mrs. Jennings had failed her in pursuing every detail with her curious questions, or with revealing it. Elinor thought Miss Steele had spoken of Edward in a negative way, suggesting that she knew a secret of his. However, no matter how often Edward's name was spoken, Miss Steele did not take any more notice of it.

Chapter Twenty-Two

Marianne did not have tolerance for vulgar people, or even those who had a different taste to hers, and so was not pleased with the Miss Steele sisters at all. She did not encourage their friendship and remained cold to them. Lucy was clever, and Elinor could deal with her for half an hour, but she was also uneducated and illiterate. This could not be hidden from Elinor, who saw she lacked even general knowledge. Elinor pitied her, but not enough to be friends with her. One day, Lucy and Elinor were walking together from Barton Park to the cottage, and she asked Elinor if she personally knew Mrs. Ferrars. Elinor thought the question was odd, but admitted she had never met Mrs. Ferrars. Lucy had assumed she'd visited Norland while Elinor was still there, and was sorry she could not tell Lucy what kind of a woman she was. Elinor, conscious of her real opinion of Mrs. Ferrars, kept quiet. Lucy revealed there were specific reasons for why she asked after Mrs. Ferrars, and hoped that she would not be seen as impolite for keeping them to herself. They continued on again in silence until Lucy broke it by once again expressing her desire to not be seen as impolite: she did not want Elinor—someone who she respected and looked up to—having a bad opinion of her. She reveals she is in an uncomfortable situation, and does not want to involve or trouble Elinor. Elinor is sorry she cannot help Lucy, but did not know she was connected to the family at all. She is surprised that Lucy asked for such a serious opinion of Mrs. Ferrars. Lucy did not blame her for being surprised. She admits that they are not connected at all at the present moment, but she believed that in time, they would be intimately connected. Lucy blushed and looked down when she admitted this. Elinor immediately hinted that Lucy might be engaged to Robert Ferrars, but Lucy denies this! She is engaged to his elder brother! Elinor was surprised and in pain. She said nothing, unable to say a single word, and tried to be strong. Lucy knows it is a surprise to her: they have kept it a secret, and told no one until she told Elinor. She has only mentioned it to Elinor because she knows she can depend on her to keep a secret, and to explain her odd questions about Mrs. Ferrars. Elinor finally spoke and, in a calm voice that even surprised her, asked how long the engagement had existed. Lucy reveals they have been engaged for four years! Elinor struggles to hide her surprise. She mentions that she did not even know Lucy and Edward knew each other until the other day. Lucy tells her that Edward was under her Uncle's care for a long while. Her Uncle, Mr Pratt, has been mentioned by Edward a few times. He lived with Mr. Pratt for four years in Plymouth, which is where their friendship began and where the engagement was formed. She was unwilling to accept Edward at first, because his mother knew nothing about her, but she was young and so in love. She begs Elinor to realize how good Edward is at making a woman fall in love with him, and that she certainly had no choice. Lucy doesn't know the half of it, but Elinor only expresses her surprise. At first, she doesn't know why Edward never mentioned Lucy's name, but then realizes it would have drawn suspicion over their friendship if he had. Lucy did not know how much longer they would have to wait, but knows it hurts Edward. She hands her a small portrait, which she has carried for three years. Elinor does not want to even look at Edward's picture, and returns it to Lucy immediately. Lucy asks her to keep the engagement a secret. Elinor will keep it a secret, but wonders why she has told someone else and threatened the secret's safety. Lucy feels that they are old friends, even though they have only just met, and wanted her advice on the matter. Her sister, Anne, knows about it, but Lucy is always afraid that she might let the secret slip. When Edward's name was mentioned a few days prior, Lucy was sure Anne would hint at the engagement. Lucy starts to cry a little here, but Elinor did not feel sorry for her. Lucy admitted that she has considered breaking off the engagement with him because it might be best for the both of them, but cannot make him miserable. She loves him too much, but knows how much stress both of them are under. Elinor cannot give her advice—Lucy must follow her own judgement. Lucy agrees. She asks Elinor if she thought Edward was depressed—he was sad when he left the Steeples sisters to visit Barton. He had stayed with them for two weeks before he came to the Dashwoods—Elinor remembered Edward had told them he'd stayed with friends, but had not mentioned anything specific about them. Elinor agreed that he seemed sad when he arrived. Lucy asks her to look over a letter she received before she left Exeter to see if she thinks he is still depressed. Elinor is certain that Lucy has not made a mistake. She considered Lucy might have been given Edward's portrait by accident, but the letter is firm proof of their engagement. While Elinor is overcome by her own emotion for a moment, she recovers to prevent suspicion. Lucy reveals that she had given Edward a ring with a lock of her hair threaded through it, and wonders if Elinor noticed it. She had: Elinor tries to compose herself, despite the distress she felt. Thankfully they had reached the cottage, and the conversation had to come to an end. After a while, the Steele returned to the Park and left an unhappy Elinor in their wake.

Chapter Twenty-Three

While Elinor could have suspected various elements in Lucy's story, she found that she could not. There was no reason why she would have made up the story when so much of it could be verified by certain things Edward had already alluded to in the past. The only contradiction to the story were her own wishes that it was untrue. Everything else pointed to it being true: his staying with Mr. Pratt, Lucy's Uncle, his sad state of mind when he visited Barton, his uncertain and changing behaviour toward Elinor, the picture, letter and ring, and both the Steele sister's knowledge of Norland and the Dashwood family connections. Elinor's thoughts led her to wonder if Edward had been deceiving her on purpose. If he pretended to love her, and felt nothing for her. Elinor could not be persuaded that he did not love her—everyone at Norland recognized his affection for her when they were at Norland, so she had not imagined it. Edward was at fault for remaining at Norland, and leading her on while he knew he could never marry Elinor. Even though Elinor could not forgive Edward for the way he treated her, she still felt sorry for him. She wondered how he would ever be happy with a wife like Lucy—someone illiterate, selfish and manipulative. His infatuation four years earlier might have blinded him from her true personality and flaws. Lucy, even lower in status than Elinor, would be much more difficult match for Edward's mother to approve. As she considered these points, she cried for Edward more than for herself. She had to protect the secret and could not arouse the suspicion of her sisters or mother. Elinor made sure that when she came to dinner she seemed perfectly fine, even though it had only been two hours since she found her heart broken. Elinor was relieved that she could keep Lucy and Edward's engagement a secret. It meant she did not have to hurt her family with the truth. Elinor would not have to listen to them talk badly about Edward, either, which they would do because of their dedication to one of their own. Neither her sisters or mother could have provided her with any help in this situation. She was stronger by herself.

Although she had suffered through the first conversation with Lucy about Edward, she wanted to continue it. She wanted to hear the specific details of their engagement to one another, and to understand what Lucy really felt for Edward. She wanted to be sure that Lucy was sincere and that Edward was not being led on. Elinor also wanted to express her interest in this subject as only a friend and nothing more; she knew Lucy suspected she was interested in Edward, especially after reacting with distress when the subject was first mentioned. Elinor was sure Lucy was jealous of her: Edward had clearly complimented Elinor in front of Lucy. Lucy's trust in her was enough evidence of that. Elinor considered, too, that Edward must have been in love with her and that Lucy suspected it and was jealous. There was no other reason for Lucy to tell Elinor about their engagement other than to encourage her to avoid Edward. She had the prior claim on her. While Elinor was determined to avoid Edward, to keep to the principles of honourable behaviour, she also wanted to convince Lucy that she was not hurt by the news. She had already heard the news—the worst that she *could* hear—so Elinor could listen to it for a second time without reacting negatively.

However, there was not an opportunity for them to talk again immediately. The weather was bad, which meant that they could not go for a walk to separate themselves from the rest of the group. There had been two meetings as a group without Elinor having a chance to talk to Lucy in private when Sir John visited the cottage one morning. He apologized for missing dinner with them that night. He would be leaving them alone with Lady Middleton, Mrs. Jennings and the two Steele sisters. Elinor immediately accepted the invitation to dinner, foreseeing a chance to talk to Lucy. Margaret agreed to attend, too, and Marianne—even though she had to be persuaded—finally gave in. Lady Middleton was thankful that the Dashwood sisters turned up—they saved her from a boring night. Elinor was correct in her estimation of the night: it was tedious and uninteresting. However, after they had dinner, cards were arranged on a table for a game, and Elinor began to wonder why she had ever thought she might find time to talk to Lucy alone. Lady Middleton hinted to Lucy that she might finish making Annamaria's basket so her daughter wouldn't be disappointed the following day. After candles are brought in for Lucy to see her work, she sits by herself, pretending to be excited about working on the basket. Lady Middleton then asked who wanted to play cards, and no one made an objection, except for Marianne who would rather play the pianoforte than cards. She hates cards. Lady Middleton is shocked by Marianne's honesty, and Elinor is left to smooth over her sister's insult. Elinor suggested that she might be useful to Lucy, especially as there was so much work left to do that Lucy was probably not going to finish it that night. Lucy, wanting Elinor's help, agreed that there was a lot more work than she first thought and did not want to disappoint Annamaria. Lady Middleton was pleased that she would be able to help, and Elinor got her own way without insulting Lady Middleton. It was something that Marianne had not learnt to do yet. While Marianne played the pianoforte, Elinor was sure that her conversation with Lucy would not be heard by those playing cards.

Chapter Twenty-Four

Elinor started the conversation by insisting she would be undeserving of Lucy's confidence in her if she did not ask anymore questions. She refused to apologize for bringing it up. Lucy, happy that Elinor brought the subject up again, had been worried she had offended Elinor by the news. Elinor had not wanted Lucy to believe that. Lucy assured her that Elinor had reacted in a cold, displeased way, and had made Lucy uncomfortable. She was sure Elinor was angry with her, and had been beating herself up for telling Elinor since. Lucy was glad it was just her paranoia and imagination playing tricks on her. She is relieved to have someone to speak to about Edward as it is the only thing on her mind. Elinor understands the need to tell someone. She sympathizes with Lucy and her difficult situation, particularly because of Edward's dependence on his mother. Lucy admits he only has two thousand pounds, which would not be enough to get married with. She could give up everything for him and live in poverty, but did not want to rob Edward of the inheritance he might receive from his mother in the future. Lucy knew that they would have to wait—for many years still, even. Lucy depends on Edward's constant affection for her, and knows he depends on her's. Elinor agrees: if their attachment had failed, Lucy's situation would be difficult. Lucy admits that Edward's love for her has been tested since their engagement and has survived. She does not doubt him now. Lucy admits she has a fairly jealous personality, and would have been able to discover anything deceitful Edward was doing. She is an observant person and looks for hints in his behaviour—so much so that she does not think she could be deceived by him at all. Lucy asks for Elinor's opinion—if she agrees with Lucy that she has to wait for Mrs. Ferrars' death, however morbid that might seem. Elinor admits that Mrs. Ferrars is a proud woman, and might be angry enough when she heard of the engagement to leave everything to Robert instead.

Elinor then asked if she knew Robert Ferrars. She has never personally met him, but has heard he is the opposite to Edward. Miss Steele overhears the end of this conversation because Marianne had stopped playing. She assumes they are talking about their "beauxs" because Lucy referred to Robert as a "great coxcomb". Lucy insists that their "beauxs" are not coxcombs. Mrs. Jennings knows that Miss Dashwood's "beaux" is a remarkably well behaved man, but does not even know who Lucy's is. Miss Steele suggested that both Lucy and Elinor's "beauxs" are remarkably similar. Elinor blushed. Lucy flashed an angry look at her sister.

After a little silence, during which Marianne began loudly playing the piano again, Lucy spoke quietly to Elinor about her idea. She knows Edward prefers the Church for his profession. She thinks he should take orders as soon as he can. Elinor, and John Dashwood, might be able to help him get a place in the Norland parish, which is meant to be a good one. This would give Lucy and Edward a chance to marry and support themselves rather than waiting for his mother to die. Elinor would be happy to help, and pointed out that Edward was John's wife's brother, which should be more than enough support for Edward. Lucy suggested that Mrs. John Dashwood would not approve of Edward working in a parish. Elinor would not be able to do anything, then. Lucy wonders if the wisest way to approach this situation would be breaking off the engagement with Edward. There are so many difficulties for them that it might be for the best. She asks for Elinor's advice, but she refuses to give it. She knows Lucy would not take her advice unless it supported her own views. Lucy thinks this is insulting—she thinks so highly of Elinor's judgement that, if she were advised to, she would break off the engagement with Edward immediately. Elinor was embarrassed, but admitted she would be too frightened to give her advice if this was the amount of power she wielded over Lucy. Lucy insisted it was only because Elinor was indifferent that her judgement would have so much power. If Lucy suspected Elinor had a personal interest or bias in the matter, her opinion and judgement would not be worth hearing. Elinor decided not to answer this, and they both descended into a silence.

Lucy asked if she would be in town that winter. Elinor would not be. Lucy was sorry to hear that, as she would have loved to see them there. She was, however, sure that John Dashwood would invite them. Elinor would not be able to accept their invitation even if they did—it is not her decision to make. Lucy had depended on being able to spend time with them there. She and her sister are visiting relatives, but Lucy is only going to see Edward. If he was not going to be there, she would have no desire to see London. Elinor was called back to the card table, then, as a new game was about to start. Elinor had been persuaded by her conversation with Lucy that Edward was not in love with her, and would never be happy with her if they were married. From this moment on, Elinor never brought the subject up again, even though Lucy constantly brought it up if she had the chance to inform her confidante that she had recived a letter from Edward. She dismissed these conversations as soon as she could politely do so because she did not think Lucy deserved to be indulged in them.

The visit of the Steele sisters had been extended far beyond what the original invitation had specified. Although they had people in Exeter to visit, they were asked to stay on for nearly two months at Barton Park.

Chapter Twenty-Five

Although Mrs. Jennings spent most of the year at Barton Park, she did have her own house. When her husband died, she began spending every winter in a house in the streets near Portman Square. As January approached, Mrs. Jennings began to think more seriously about leaving Barton for London until one day she unexpectedly asked both the older Miss Dashwoods to come with her. Elinor, ignoring the animated and excited Marianne, declined the invitation for the both of them because they did not want to leave their mother alone. Mrs. Jennings was surprised by their rejection and invited them again immediately. She insisted that Mrs. Dashwood would be fine without them, that they would not be inconveniencing Mrs. Jennings at all because she wanted them to come, and they could do as they pleased when they were in town. Mrs. Jennings believed Mrs. Dashwood would be more than happy for them to go to town, particularly as Mrs. Jennings had such an easy time marrying off her own children that at least one of the Dashwood sisters would be married before they returned from town. Sir John interjected then, and pointed out that Marianne—if Elinor was not involved— would have agreed to go. As it was unfair for Marianne to have to suffer because of Elinor, he suggested that Mrs. Jennings and she should simply leave Barton without telling anyone where they are going. Mrs. Jennings thought it would be best if they came together so they would have someone besides her to talk to. Still, she will take either or both of them, and asks Marianne to shake her hand to agree on the invitation. Marianne insists that the invitation has made her truly happy, and would make her happier if she accepted it, but she understands and agrees with what Elinor has said about their mother. Elinor now realized that Marianne wanted to go to speak with and see Willoughby, and said nothing more to object to the plan. She merely let her mother make the decision. Generally, whatever Marianne wanted, their mother agreed with, and she did not believe she had the ability to sway her mother in the other direction. That Marianne, who was generally disgusted with Mrs. Jenning's manners, was willing to go with her to London spoke for how excited Marianne was by this invitation. Elinor could not oppose her, even if she wanted to avoid seeing Edward in London. When Mrs. Dashwood heard about the invitation, she would not let them decline it because they were worried about her. She insisted that they both accept it. She believed both she and Margaret would benefit from their travels, too. When the Middletons were gone, she and Margaret would work together on her education and refinement. She also had plans for altering their bedrooms, which could be carried out while they were away. She was pleased that they would have a motherly Mrs. Jennings to look after them, and that they would most likely see their brother, John Dashwood, while they were there. Elinor only had one objection to voice, which was Mrs. Jenning's awful manners. Marianne did not want to reject the invitation, even if Elinor would. Elinor couldn't help but smile at Marianne's determination. If Marianne would go, Elinor would too. She did not want to leave Marianne alone without her guidance. In fact, Elinor believed it was possible their visit might be over by the time Edward managed to visit London in February. Mrs. Dashwood suggested that Elinor might be able to improve her friendship with her future family; Elinor wished that Mrs. Dashwood would stop connecting her and Edward together, and voiced her opinion that, although she liked Edward and would always be glad to see him, she did not care for the rest of the family. Marianne was surprised!

The invitation was accepted. Mrs. Jennings was overjoyed, and Sir John was delighted that he would have more friends in London. Lady Middleton even took time to look delighted, which was unlike her, and Lucy had never been happier. Marianne was more than happy. Her only objection to going to London was leaving her mother, and at the moment they left, her grief was excessive. Mrs. Dashwood shared in this emotion, and it seemed to Elinor that she was the only one of three who did not think of the separation as permanent. They left in the first week of January, with the Middletons and Steele sisters following the week after.

Chapter Twenty-Six

Elinor was a little surprised to find herself in a carriage and under the care of someone they had not been friends with for long and who was totally unsuited to their age and manners. However, the happiness and excitement Marianne had been wrapped up in allowed Elinor to overlook this. Despite Elinor's occasional doubts in Willoughby, she could not deny Marianne the joy that swept across her face. This joy, however, also reminded her of how blank and sad her own mind was. She decided to focus on Marianne to feel hope once more. Elinor knew to expect Willoughby in London already—Marianne's eagerness to leave more than suggested she had heard the same—and she hoped to uncover new estimations of his personality to better understand him and his intentions toward Marianne. She would attempt to lead Marianne away from him if she heard unfavourable accounts of Willoughby.

Their journey to London took three days, during which Marianne barely spoke—so wrapped up in excitement and nerves that she was unable to. Elinor was left to atone for her sister's behaviour and talked and laughed with Mrs. Jennings throughout the journey.

When they finally reached London, they were happy to leave the carriage. The house was pretty, and the two Dashwood sisters were immediately given a comfortable room. Dinner was two hours away still, so Elinor decided to write to their mother. Marianne sat down to write, too. Elinor insisted she put off her own letter home until a little later, but Marianne was not writing to their mother. She didn't say anything else, but Elinor knew that she was writing to Willoughby. She concluded that they must be engaged to be mysteriously writing to each other, and Elinor was pleased. Marianne completed her letter in a few minutes and had it taken away to be delivered immediately. Throughout the rest of the day, Marianne was nervous and seemed to be anxious listening for visitors. Mrs. Jennings seemed unaware of everything that was going on, being distracted by her own house, and Elinor was thankful for it. Finally, a knock at their door seemed to signal Willoughby's arrival. Elinor was sure of it. Marianne left the room to listen for who it was, and after listening for a moment returned in a fluster. She was sure it was Willoughby, and was about to throw herself into his arms when Colonel Brandon stepped in! Marianne could not bear the shock and left the room immediately. Elinor was disappointed, too, but her friendship with Colonel Brandon made her sympathize with him. That a man so in love with Marianne should think that she experienced only grief when she saw him was upsetting. Colonel Brandon asked if Marianne was ill. Elinor answered that she was, and mentioned enough symptoms to explain Marianne's behaviour. They started to talk of other general things, but Elinor only wanted to ask him if Willougby was in London. She did not want to cause Brandon pain by asking after his rival. She asked, instead, if he had been in London since he left Barton. He admitted, with embarrassment, that he had. He had been unable to return to Barton. This reminded Elinor of the way he left, and the suspicion Mrs. Jennings had felt during the situation. Elinor feared that her question might have implied much more curiosity about his escape to London than she actually felt.

Mrs. Jennings stepped in and welcomed Brandon. She asked how Brandon knew that they back in London that day, and he reveals he heard it from the Palmers. He had just been to dinner there. Mrs. Jennings asked after Mrs. Palmer—she is sure that Mrs. Palmer is extremely pregnant by now. Brandon reveals Mrs. Jennings will see her tomorrow. Mrs. Jennings mentions that she has brought Marianne and Elinor with her and suggests he and Willoughby will need to work out what they are going to do about Marianne. She then asks him what he has been doing in London since they last saw one another, and Brandon answers in his usually vague but polite way. Marianne returned, obliged to appear again. Brandon became immediately more thoughtful and silent and did not stay long. No other visitors arrived, and the Dashwood sisters had to go to bed.

Marianne rose the next morning with renewed hope. She had seemed to forget the disappointment of the previous day. Mrs. Palmer arrived at the house, happy and surprised to see the Dashwood sisters there. She was angry that they had rejected her invitation, but accepted her mother's, but forgave them because they came anyway. After a few hours of conversation, Mrs. Palmer asked them to come shopping with her—an invitation which was enthusiastically accepted. Wherever they went, Marianne kept a watchful eye out for Willoughby. She was restless and distracted, and could not give opinions on any of the purchases being made, even if it concerned her too. She did not seem to enjoy herself, and seemed impatient to get back to the house again. It was late when they arrived back, and Marianne flew upstairs to see if Willoughby had visited. He had not, and there were no letters or notes for her. Marianne thought it was odd, and turned to look out of the door. Elinor agreed but kept her thoughts to herself. Marianne knew he was in town, which is why she had written to him, so Elinor did not understand why he would not come to visit. She longed to ask Marianne about the engagement, but did not know how the question would be received by her sister. Elinor decided that if more of these unpleasant days followed, she would strongly suggest to her mother to step in and question Marianne.

Later on that evening, while a few visitors played whist with Elinor and Mrs. Jennings, Marianne could not relax. She spent the entire evening in the depths of anxious expectation, and the pain of her disappointment.

Chapter Twenty-Seven

Mrs. Jennings told them all that Sir John might not leave Barton Park the next week because the weather was so good and would keep them in the country. Marianne agreed: she had not thought of that at all. She hoped that the rain would come soon, though and in a few days—maybe even that night—the weather would turn cold. Elinor wanted to shield Mrs. Jennings from Marianne's true meaning, and changed the subject. Elinor believed Marianne would write to Willoughby at Combe that day, but if Marianne did, Elinor did not see it. Marianne was happy all day, especially with her expectation of a frost that evening. She commented on the weather while they carried out errands, believing that there was a sudden change in it.

Colonel Brandon was with them almost every day so he could look at Marianne and talk to Elinor. Elinor was pleased to talk to him, but grew more concerned for his state of mind. She was afraid that Brandon's love for Marianne was strengthening, not weakening, and she was sorry for it. About a week after they had arrived, a card came from Willoughby to announce he was in town. Marianne was horrified he had visited while they were out of the house, but Elinor assured her he would return the following day. While the arrival of the card made Elinor happier, it threw Marianne back into her anguished state. She insisted on staying behind the next morning while everyone else went out. When Elinor returned she only had to look at Marianne to know Willoughby had not paid a second visit. A letter came, then, and Marianne thought it might be for her. It was a note for Mrs. Jennings. Elinor asked if Marianne was expecting a letter, but her response was vague. Elinor accused her of not trusting her, and Marianne returned the accusation. Elinor was confused and assured Marianne she had nothing to tell her. Marianne insisted the same was true for her, too. Mrs. Jennings read the letter out: Lady Middleton had written to announce their arrival in London the night before. She had invited them to the house to pay a visit as both Sir John's business and Lady Middleton's cold prevented them from coming to Mrs. Jennings. The invitation was accepted, but as the time drew near for them to leave, Elinor could not persuade her sister to go. She did not want to run the risk of missing Willoughby again and wanted to stay behind in the house, but Marianne was not allowed to stay behind. When they arrived at the Middleton house, they found Sir John had decided to throw an impromptu ball. Lady Middleton was not pleased because she did not think she was prepared enough to throw a respectable ball. After an hour or so, Mr. Palmer told Elinor he thought they were still in Devonshire. This surprised Elinor because she knew Brandon and Mrs. Palmer had told him they were in London. On the way back to Mrs. Jenning's house, Marianne complained that the dancing had made her tired. Mrs. Jennings joked that if a certain person, namely Willoughby, had been there, she would not have been tired at all. She thinks it was strange that Willoughby did not come even though Sir John had invited him earlier that day. Marianne said nothing else but looked hurt. Elinor decided to write to their mother the next day out of fear for Marianne, hoping she might step in and ask the questions that needed asking. Her letter was barely finished when Colonel Brandon arrived. Marianne, seeing him arrive, left the room. Brandon looked troubled and sat without saying a word for quite some time. He looked like he needed to say something in particular, and Elinor was impatient for him to begin. After a moment, Brandon asked Elinor if he should congratulate her on her new brother. Elinor did not know what he meant. Brandon told her that Marianne's engagement to Willoughby was exceedingly well known. Elinor disagreed. Not even her family knew about it. Brandon revealed that the engagement was talked about my many people including Mrs. Jennings, Mrs. Palmer, and the Middletons. He would not have believed it until he saw a letter addressed to Willoughby from Marianne leave the house that day. Brandon asked if everything was settled and agreed on, in case he might continue to hope for what he thought was impossible: Marianne's hand in marriage. Elinor could not say anything at first, and debated what she should say. Elinor did not actually know what the state of things between Willoughby and Marianne actually were, so she did not know what exactly to say. However, she knew that Marianne's affection for Willoughby meant that Colonel Brandon had no chance. She decided to say more than she actually knew for certain, to prevent his continuing hope: she told him that even though she did not know the exact terms of their agreement, she knew they were in love with another and was not surprised to hear they were writing to one another. Brandon stood then, and wished Marianne happiness, and hoped that Willoughby would try to deserve her. He left. Elinor was uneasy: Colonel Brandon's unhappiness and Elinor's need to confirm the engagement which caused it made her anxious and worried for Marianne and for the future.

Chapter Twenty-Eight

Nothing happened in the next three or four days to make Elinor regret writing to her mother. Willoughby did not visit or write to Marianne. They had to attend a party with Lady Middleton one night without Mrs. Jennings. Marianne did not care where she went, or what she looked like, and so sat by the drawing room fire after tea until Lady Middleton arrived to take them away. She was lost in her thoughts, and was not aware Lady Middleton had arrived until Elinor roused her.

They arrived at the party into a room lit up, full of people and intensely hot. When they had said their polite greetings to the hosts of the party, they mingled with the crowd. Lady Middleton sat down to a card game, and Marianne and Elinor sat nearby to watch, unwilling to do anything else. They had not been sitting there for long until Elinor noticed Willoughby talking to a fashionable young woman. Elinor caught his eye, and he bowed but made no attempt to speak to them or approach them. He carried on his conversation with the young woman. Elinor turned to Marianne to see if she had noticed him, and as she did, Elinor grabbed her before she could move toward him. Marianne did not know why she could not go and speak to him, and Elinor insisted she behave herself just in case others could see how she felt about him. Marianne could not compose herself. Willoughby turned around and looked at them both. Marianne stood, and held out her hand to him. He approached them but talked mostly to Elinor than to Marianne, as if he wanted to avoid looking at her. He asked how long they had been in town. Elinor could not say a word, but Marianne expressed her feelings: she wondered why Willoughby would not shake her hand, or if he had not received her letters. Willoughby was struggling to compose himself. Marianne, at the height of anxiety, begged him to tell her what was wrong with him. He made no reply, caught the eye of the young lady he was speaking with, and turned away after thanking them for sending a note of their arrival in London.

Marianne sunk into a chair. Elinor thought she might faint and tried to hide her from others. She gave her some water to prevent her from fainting. Marianne begged Elinor to bring Willoughby to her so she could speak with him. She wanted an explanation. Elinor told her to wait until the next day for an explanation. Elinor struggled to keep Marianne from following Willoughby herself, and to keep this situation private, but she continued to complain and express her feelings. Elinor saw Willoughby leave, and told Marianne he had gone and that she would not be able to talk to Willoughby at all. Marianne begged Elinor to persuade Lady Middleton to let them go home. When Lady Middleton was told Marianne was feeling unwell, they left as soon as the carriage could be found. Marianne said nothing. She didn't even cry—she was too upset to cry. Once home, Marianne went straight to bed and Elinor sat up waiting for Mrs. Jennings to return.

Elinor did not doubt that there had been an understanding between Willoughby and Marianne. Although Marianne tended to feed her own wishes and emotions, there was no doubt that Willoughby had encouraged it, and then changed his feelings toward her. Although their parting might have dulled their attachment to one another, it could not explain the drastic change in Willoughby. Elinor thought she was quite lucky. She could still admire Edward, even though she had lost him, but Willoughby was utterly lost to Marianne, even as a friend.

Chapter Twenty-Nine

Early the next morning, Marianne—half dressed—was knelt against one of the window seats writing as fast as her tears would allow her. Elinor woke up to the sounds of Marianne sobbing. After watching her for a while, she wondered if she might ask Marianne what she was doing. Marianne told her to wait and ask nothing because she would know everything soon. Elinor was certain that Marianne was writing her last letter to Willoughby. Whereas she would usually have tried to sooth Marianne, she left her alone because Marianne had asked her so seriously. Marianne dressed and could not stay in the room any longer. She wandered around the house until breakfast, avoiding everyone. At breakfast, she ate nothing, and Elinor tried to keep Mrs. Jennings occupied. They had just left the breakfast table when a letter was delivered to Marianne. She turned pale and ran out of the room. Elinor knew the letter had come from Willoughby, and felt quite sick. Mrs. Jennings only noticed that Marianne had received a letter from Willoughby, and hoped that she liked what it said. Mrs. Jennings had never seen a girl so in love. Not even her daughters were affected as much as Marianne is. She hoped that Willoughby would not keep her waiting too much longer, and asked Elinor when the wedding would be held. Elinor assured her that she had no idea why the joke of Marianne's engagement to Willoughby was now being taken seriously. She told Mrs. Jennings that they were not to be married. Mrs. Jennings did not believe her on account of how in love they were with one another, and believed that Marianne had come to London to buy wedding clothes. She admits she has told anyone who will listen about it. Elinor tells her she is unkind to be spreading a rumour like this.

Elinor left the room, eager to find out what Willoughby had written. Marianne, sobbing, was stretched across the bed with the letter in her hands. Elinor kissed her and then burst into tears herself. Marianne placed the letters into Elinor's hands and then hid behind her handkerchief. Elinor read the letter. Willoughby apologizes for any behaviour which might have offended her and asks for her forgiveness on this count. He also expresses his respect and affection for the Dashwood family, but regrets if he gave Marianne the wrong idea about the extent of his feelings for her. He cannot be any more to her than a friend as he has been in love for a long time with someone else and will be engaged within a few weeks. He has sent Marianne's letters back to her at her request. Elinor was struck by the dishonour and indelicacy Willoughby was capable of. She felt his letter was cruel, and ungentlemanly—he had denied his affection for her, and not acknowledged any true regret for knowingly leading Marianne on. Elinor hated the man, but did not speak in case she upset Marianne any more.

When Elinor heard a carriage pulling up to the house, she went to the window to see who it was who had arrived at the house so early. It was Mrs. Jennings's carriage, which she knew had not been ordered until later. She rushed to find Mrs. Jennings and make her excuses, hoping to stay behind with Marianne and look after her. Mrs. Jennings let her stay behind, and Elinor returned to Marianne in time to prevent her from fainting on the floor due to lack of rest and food. Elinor found her a glass of wine and put her back in bed. Elinor wished she could do more to help her. Marianne accused Elinor of being unable to know how she felt. Elinor was not happy! She could not be while she saw Marianne so upset. Marianne hugged her, but knew she had to be happy. Edward loved her, and nothing could take away Elinor's happiness because of that. Elinor changed the subject— she pointed out that Marianne was lucky. She might have suffered for months on end until his true nature was finally revealed and the engagement broken off. Marianne told her there was no engagement. Willoughby had not broken any promises with her. Elinor is surprised. She asked if Willoughby told her he loved her. He did not express it but implied it every day. Elinor turned her attention to the letters Willoughby had returned to Marianne. The first told him that they had arrived in London and that she expected a visit from him. The second expressed her disappointment and surprise that he had not replied to her note yet. The last, written the morning after their meeting at the party, demanded an explanation for his behaviour. Elinor knew that Marianne had crossed a line: her letters were impolite and revealed much more of her feelings than she should have revealed to him. Marianne felt she had been treated cruelly, but not by Willoughby. Instead, every one of their acquaintances had grouped together to ruin her in his opinion. The woman he wrote about—the one he loved—might be anyone. She did not know why she should trust anyone else in the world beyond her own family and Edward. Elinor suggests that she show this person that she is not hurt by it, and to hold her head up high, but Marianne cannot show any semblance of pride. She does not care who knows she is upset. She could not appear happy when in reality she is miserable.

Marianne wondered where Willoughby's heart had gone. She wondered if he could be justified in his treatment of her. Elinor denied this: he could not. Marianne did not know who this other woman could be as Willoughby had never mentioned a young, attractive woman as his friend to them. She wanted to go home tomorrow. She only came to London for Willoughby's sake, and there was no reason for her to be there anymore. Elinor could not agree: they would not be able to leave so soon. Mrs. Jennings deserved far more polite behaviour, and this would take a few more days at least. Marianne was worried about what the Palmers and Middletons would say, and did not think she could deal with their remarks and jokes. Elinor told her to lie down again and, after Marianne grows agitated, retrieves some lavender drops to help her lie quietly and still.

Chapter Thirty

Mrs. Jennings came to their room as soon as she returned. She looked concerned. She had heard that Willoughby was going to be married to another woman, and Mrs. Jennings hates him for it. Mrs. Taylor told Mrs. Jennings about it, who heard it from a friend of Miss Grey, the woman meant to marry him. Mrs. Jennings would not have believed it had she not heard about it from someone involved. She told Mrs. Taylor that Willoughby had treated a young lady friend badly, and hoped that his new wife would destroy his heart. If she meets with Willoughby, she is determined to tell him off. She tries to comfort Marianne with the knowledge that there were plenty of other young men in the world, and with Marianne's pretty face, she'll have plenty of admirers. After telling Elinor that the Parrys and Sandersons were visiting that night, she left them to mourn alone.

Marianne was determined to have dinner with the rest of the group that night. Elinor advised her not to, but she wanted to go down so people could stop fussing over her. Elinor was pleased that this was the reason she wanted to go down, and said nothing else even though she did not think Marianne could last the dinner. Marianne was far calmer and ate more than Elinor thought she might be. If she actually spoke, or if Mrs. Jenning's made a poor comment, she was sure that Marianne would have started to cry. Elinor was grateful to Mrs. Jennings for treating her sister with kindness. She indulged and fussed over Marianne, asking sure she had he best place by the fire, was offered treats to eat and amused her with the good news of the day. It seemed as if Mrs. Jennings thought the cure for disappointment in love was an abundance of treats. As soon as Marianne realized this is what Mrs. Jennings was doing, Marianne left the room.

Mrs. Jennings was upset that Marianne was so depressed and that none of the treats she were given helped her. If she knew what would help cure her sadness, she would have it brought to Marianne right away. Elinor asked if Miss Grey, the lady Willoughby was engaged to, was rich. She was, with fifty thousand pounds to her name and a smart, but not beautiful girl. Mrs. Jennings thinks Willoughby is need of money, but this doesn't give him the right to pretend to be in love with Marianne, and then drop her when a richer girl wants to marry him. Mrs. Jennings had never heard anything bad about Miss Grey except that her guardians, Mr. and Mrs. Ellison, did not get on well with her and would be glad to have her married. Miss Grey, being of age, has been able to decide who she wants to marry. Mrs. Jennings suggests that they play one of Marianne's favourite games to entice her out of her room. Although Elinor thanks her for her kindness, she knows Marianne won't come out of her room again that evening. Elinor will suggest she goes to sleep early. Mrs. Jennings had no idea that Marianne was going through all of this, and would not have joked about it if she had had an idea. Elinor suggests that she won't need to tell Mrs. Palmer and Sir John not to mention Willoughby's name or mention anything to do with what had happened in front of Marianne. She does not think that they would be so cruel. Mrs. Jennings will hint that they need to be careful around Marianne, especially as she believes the less that is said on the matter, the better. Elinor must do Willoughby some justice, however, and admits he has broken no official engagement with Marianne as there was none. Mrs. Jennings tells her not to defend him, especially after his behaviour and taking her to Allenham House to see her future rooms.

Mrs. Jennings suggests that Colonel Brandon will be able to ask Marianne to marry him, and doubts that it will take long for them to marry. It will be a much better match for Marianne, anyway. She hopes that they will be able to drive Willoughby out of Marianne's head to make room for Brandon. Elinor just hopes that they can drive Willoughby out, with or without Brandon. She left Mrs. Jennings to see to Marianne, who was leaning over a small fire. After Elinor successfully sent Marianne to bed, she returned to Mrs. Jennings in the drawing room, where they shared a glass of wine. Colonel Brandon came in, then, and looked around for Marianne. Elinor did not think he expected to find her there, and knew that he had heard what had happened, but Mrs. Jennings did not think he knew anything as he looked so serious. Brandon, with a look that implied he knew exactly how she was, asked after Marianne. Elinor admitted she had been unwell. Brandon stepped carefully and, in a roundabout way, asked if what he had heard that morning had been true. Elinor admitted it was true. She asked where he had heard the news. Brandon had been at a stationer's shop, running some errands, when he overheard two ladies talking about it. One of the ladies had been Mrs. Ellison, Miss Grey's guardian. Elinor suggested Willoughby was only marrying her for the money. Brandon started to say something on the matter, and then stopped. They discussed Marianne's current condition. Elinor hoped that her grief would be short. She thought that Marianne had been deceived by Willoughby, but Marianne would justify anything he did if she could still do so. Brandon dropped the subject. Mrs. Jennings was amazed that Brandon was not a happier man for hearing the news, and actually appeared more serious and thoughtful than he usually was.

Chapter Thirty-One

When Marianne woke, she woke to the same thoughts of Willoughby's betrayal that had sent her to bed. Elinor encouraged her to talk about it as much as she could, and before breakfast they had gone over the events multiple times. Marianne's feelings varied: sometimes she could scarcely believe Willoughby's betrayal, and other times she was angry with him for deceiving her. Marianne was certain of one thing, however, and that was avoiding Mrs. Jennings, and remaining silent when she had to be with her. Marianne truly believed that Mrs. Jennings did not feel sympathy for her but only wanted more details to gossip with. Elinor thought this was not fair to Mrs. Jennings and was only further evidence that Marianne was led astray sometimes when forming her opinions of others. Marianne only expected the same opinions and feelings in others as her own, and judged the motives of others by seeing how they directly affected her. When Mrs. Jennings stepped into the room, full of good intentions, Marianne only judged her poorly because it caused her some pain. Mrs. Jennings held a letter in her hand, which she was sure would help Marianne. Marianne's imagination was in full force. First, she imagined that the letter was from Willoughby, full of explanations and apologies. Then, she thought Willoughby might run into the room and gather at her feet, assuring her that he was in the wrong. However, she saw that the letter had her mother's handwriting on it, and her fantasies were destroyed. The cruelty she thought Mrs. Jennings had caused her made her cry, and Marianne could not find words to express how she felt. When Marianne was calm enough, she read the letter. It did not bring her comfort as the name Willoughby filled every page. Her mother was still confident that they were engaged and that Willoughby would be true to her. This letter had risen out of Elinor's plea to ask Marianne about the possible engagement, and the belief in the happy, future engagement made her sob. It also made her impatient to return home, especially as she wanted to be nearer her mother. Elinor did not know where would be best for Marianne to be, so could only ask Marianne to be patient enough to see what their mother wanted them to do. Mrs. Jennings left them to talk to the Middletons and Palmers. Elinor sat down to write to Mrs. Dashwood and tell her about everything that had happened while Marianne sat quietly and watched.

They had scarcely been sitting there for fifteen minutes when there was a knock at the door. Elinor thought they were safe from visitors. Marianne saw it was Colonel Brandon, and was upset. She retreated to her room, disagreeing that he wouldn't come in because Mrs. Jennings was not at home. Colonel Brandon had nothing to do with his time and Marianne believed nothing would keep him from coming inside. Marianne was right. Elinor was convinced that Colonel Brandon had come to visit Marianne, and noted he looked quite sad himself. Brandon admits he met with Mrs. Jennings in the street and she had encouraged him to visit. He wanted to find Elinor alone, which he has done so, so that he can tell her something more about Willoughby's character. He wants to ensure the family feels that they have had a lucky escape. Elinor is grateful to Brandon for his service to the family.

Brandon began by reminding Elinor of a conversation they had at Barton Park about a lady resembling Marianne. Elinor remembered it. Brandon believes they are similar in mind and body. She was one of his nearest relatives, an orphan, and under his father's guardianship. They were the same age, and they had been friends since they were young. He had always loved Eliza, and she had loved him. Her fortune was quite large, so to ensure the fortune remained in the family, she was married off to his brother. Brandon did not think his brother deserved her, particularly because he did not love her. Brandon hoped that her love for him would keep her spirits afloat, but they were both miserable. If her marriage to his brother had been a happy one, he might have been able to recover after a few months. However, Brandon's brother treated her unkindly. Brandon left

England to increase the distance between them. He hoped this would make her accept his brother and be happy with her marriage. Two years later, he heard about her divorce. He returned to England after three years, and failed to find her. He could not find out where she had gone after she had left his brother, and he worried she had fallen into a life of sin. She had lost most of her money, and her ex-husband suggested she had spent it all. Brandon finally found her six months after he came to England. When Brandon visited a former servant of his, who had found himself in debt, he found Eliza. She was worn down by suffering, and Brandon could hardly compare the sickly girl he saw to the beautiful, healthy girl he had once loved. She had consumption, and the only thing Brandon could do was prepare her for death. He made sure she was comfortable until her death, and Brandon was with her until the last moments. Brandon hoped that Marianne would not be offended at his comparison of her to Eliza. He knew that their fortunes would be different. Brandon promised to get to his point. He was left to care for a little girl, her child, who was about three years old then. He wanted to take care of her education himself, but he had no home or family. Little Eliza was sent to school, and Brandon visited her as often as he could. When Brandon's brother died, leaving him his fortune, Eliza visited him at Delaford. He has always called her a distant relative, but knows there are rumours which suggest he is her father. Brandon took the girl out of school three years ago so that a well respected woman in Dorsetshire could take care of her. In February—almost a year ago—she suddenly disappeared. She had gone to Bath with one of her friends who would not tell Brandon where she had gone. Brandon was left to wonder what had happened to her. Elinor interrupted to exclaim that Willoughby could not have been involved. Brandon continued. He received a letter from her in October, which he received on the morning of their abandoned party to Whitwell. This was the reason he left so suddenly. He wondered what Willoughby would have thought if he'd really known what the letter said, and if he'd realized Brandon was going to the aid of someone he had made so miserable. He did not know if Willoughby would have altered his behaviour at all, particularly when he had treated Eliza so poorly and still managed to be the happiest man in their group of friends. Willoughby had left young Eliza alone, after he seduced her, with no home, help or friends. He had promised to return but had not done so. He had not even written. Elinor is beyond shocked.

Brandon is pleased that she knows Willoughby's true nature. He has spent many weeks in distress, especially when he heard Marianne and Willoughby might be engaged. He knows that his behaviour might have seemed strange to them all, but hoped Elinor would understand why he acted the way he did. Brandon did not know what Willoughby's intentions toward Marianne were, but assumed he only meant to deceive her. Brandon hoped Marianne might be able to compare herself to Eliza and feel lucky for her escape. She might grow stronger for it. Brandon has only told her this story to help Marianne, not to complain about his past. He would have said nothing otherwise. Elinor thanked him for his help. She admits she has been annoyed with Marianne's attempts to explain Willoughby's behaviour, and this will help strengthen Marianne's mind against him. Elinor asks if Brandon has seen Willoughby since he left Barton. He had. They met so that Brandon could punish him, and Willoughby attempt to defend himself. Elinor asked if Eliza was still in London. She and her child have been taken to the country where she will remain. Brandon put an end to the visit, then, and left Elinor full of compassion for him.

Chapter Thirty-Two

When Marianne heard Brandon's story, she did not react in the way Elinor thought she might. She did not appear to doubt the story, and even treated Brandon with more kindness. She actually spoke to him, and did not avoid him when he visited. She appeared to settle down, but she was miserable. The knowledge that Willoughby was a villain was far worse for her than the loss of his heart. When Marianne thought of what Willoughby had done to poor Miss Williams, she suffered in silence. That Marianne had not told Elinor how she felt or what she thought made Elinor worry the most. Mrs. Dashwood's reply to Elinor's letter expressed the same disbelief and sorrow both the Dashwood sisters felt. Mrs. Dashwood decided that it would be far better for Marianne to avoid Barton for the time being. It was a place which would remind Marianne of her past with Willoughby. They were told not to shorten their visit to Mrs. Jennings, which was expected to last between five and six weeks. Mrs. Dashwood hoped that the variety of people and activities might give Marianne something else to focus on. She also felt that there would be little danger of Marianne bumping into Willoughby again. All of their acquaintances would have to drop him from their group of friends. She also wanted them to avoid Willoughby at Allenham, where he might go to visit his home in preparation for the wedding. Mrs. Dashwood's final reason for wanting them to stay in London was the news that her son-in-law would be in London. She wanted them to see their brother. Marianne had promised to follow her mother's advice, and gave in without opposing it, even though the orders were the exact opposite of her own wishes. Elinor secretly considered she would not be able to avoid Edward while they were still in London, but her sister's well-being was more important than her own.

While Elinor had succeeded in preventing others from mentioning Willoughby's name in front of Marianne, she had to listen to others talk about him all day, every day. Sir John did not think it was possible for a good person like Willoughby to be capable of it. He would not speak to or meet him again. Mrs. Palmer was also angry and thankful that she had never been friends with him at all. She would tell everyone she met with that he was a bad man. Unfortunately, Mrs. Palmer did not have the presence of mind to stop gossiping. Elinor soon knew all the details of Willoughby's marriage to Miss Grey, including the kind of clothes she would be wearing. Elinor was thankful for Lady Middleton's calm, polite unconcern. She was comforted that there was at least one person in their group of friends who was totally uninterested. Even though Lady Middleton stated that Willoughby had acted in a shocking manner, she was still planning on leaving a note for the future Mrs. Willoughby—a woman who would have elegance and fortune to her name.

Colonel Brandon's delicate questions regarding Marianne were not unwelcome to Elinor. He had earned the right to ask after and discuss Marianne's state of mind by his assistance. Marianne rewarded him with a sympathetic look and gentle conversation. Elinor and Brandon hoped that Marianne would continue to think of Brandon as a friend. Mrs. Jennings, believing Brandon was still depressed, thought that he and Marianne would never be married at all. In fact, she thought Brandon and Elinor might be married after all, especially as Mrs. Jennings had stopped thinking of Edward. In early February, Elinor had to announce to Marianne that Willoughby was married. Marianne did not react at once but burst into tears after a while. The Willoughbys left London. They would not bump into them, and Elinor began persuading Marianne to leave the house, which she had not done since Willoughby's first offence at the party.

By this time, the Steele sisters had arrived in London and were welcomed to Mrs. Jennings home. Elinor was sorry that they had come, especially as Lucy was so surprised they had stayed in London for more than a month. Miss Steele discusses their journey to London and a friend they made along the way. Dr. Davies, their new friend, is single, and Miss Steele is accused of going after him. Although her cousins are sure that Miss Steele and Dr. Davies like one another, Miss Steele denies it. Lucy wonders if Elinor and Marianne will stay with John Dashwood when he comes to London. Elinor denies it and is aware that Lucy is trying to hint at their previous conversations regarding Edward. Lucy declares that the Dashwoods will go, and Elinor cannot be bothered to continue arguing with her. Lucy thinks it is wonderful that Mrs. Dashwood has let her daughters stay away for so long, but Mrs. Jennings silences her with the assertion that their visit has not been long at all. Miss Steele is sorry that they could not talk with Marianne, who had left the room when the Steele sisters had arrived. Elinor assures them that Marianne would be sorry to miss them both, but has suffered with many headaches in the last little while. Miss Steele suggested Marianne could come to sit with her old friends in silence, but Elinor rejected this suggestion by hinting that Marianne was probably in bed. Miss Steele declares she will go up and see her, then. Just as Elinor was just about to lose her temper, Lucy stepped in to tell her sister off for being too pushy and impolite.

Chapter Thirty-Three

Marianne finally gave into Elinor's wishes and went out with her and Mrs. Jennings one morning. She did not want to visit anyone, and only accompanied them to a jewellers. As they arrived at the shop, Mrs. Jennings decided to go across the street to visit someone she knew while Elinor carried out her errand. The jewellers was so crowded with people that the Dashwood sisters had to wait to be served. They sat beside a gentleman, thinking that he would be done quickly. Elinor hoped his polite manners might encourage him to finish his business even faster. However, he was a perfectionist. He was ordering a toothpick case for his own use, and took fifteen minutes to examine and debate the pros and cons of every case in the shop. Because this gentleman was so engrossed in his orders for the case, he only had the time to occasionally look at the Dashwood sisters, rather than to pay proper attention to them. Elinor thought he was quite a strong, intelligent person, or at least she assumed he was from the kind of look he gave them both. Marianne was fairly ignorant to the gentleman's examination of their features and was saved from her usual resentful reaction. The gentleman finally finished his order, slowly took his gloves from the counter, looked at the Dashwood sisters in a demanding way, and walked off in a conceited way. Elinor wasted no time in finishing her own errand, and was just about to finish when another gentleman stood beside her. She was surprised to find it was John Dashwood, her brother! He was actually genuinely pleased to see them, and it gave the Dashwoods pleasure. Elinor discovered he and his wife, Fanny had been in London for two days. He had planned to visit them sooner, but had other things he had to do which took up his time. John wanted to visit them the following day so he could meet Mrs. Jennings, who he knew was a rich woman. He also wanted to meet the Middletons because they were Mrs. Dashwood's relatives and wanted to show them respect. Edward has told John that the Dashwoods are being well taken care of in Barton and that the cottage is quite charming. Elinor felt a little ashamed at the mention of Edward's name, and thankfully Mrs. Jenning's servant arrived to interrupt and retrieve them. John accompanied them to the door. He was introduced to Mrs. Jennings, and left after he expressed his hope of visiting the house the following day.

The next day, John came to the house as planned but without Fanny. She had sent her apologies for not coming. Mrs. Jennings did not mind that she had stayed behind because she was sure that they were related in some way, and wanted to seem friendly. She was sure that she would visit Mrs. John Dashwood soon anyway. John was friendly and kind to all of them and paid a lot of attention to Mrs. Jennings. When Brandon came into the room, John looked at him with curiosity. John seemed to only need a hint that Brandon was rich so that he could be civil and friendly to him, too. After half an hour, John asked Elinor to walk with him to the Middleton's home so she could introduce them to him. She agreed.

On their walk, John asked about Colonel Brandon. He wanted to know if he was a rich man, which Elinor revealed he was. John was glad because he seemed like a true gentleman. John congratulated her on the prospect of a fine match. Elinor is confused and doesn't know what John is talking about. While watching Brandon, John has become convinced that he is in love with Elinor. Elinor assures John he has made a mistake. Brandon has no intention to marry her! John insists that Brandon just needs a little more encouragement, particularly as Elinor has no fortune. If Elinor makes an effort, there's no reason why Brandon can't ignore his objections. He suggests that the entire family are eager to see her married off, particularly Fanny and Mrs. Ferrars. Elinor asks if Edward is going to be married. He is, but not everything has been agreed on just yet. Mrs. Ferrars will provide him with some money if the match is a successful one. He will be married to Miss Morton who also has money to bring to the marriage. Although Mrs. Ferrars will be under some financial pressure because of her vow to give Edward a thousand pounds a year, John only sees it as an example of her immense selflessness. She gave Fanny money when they arrived in London to cover their expenses, which John was thankful for. He reminds Elinor that their expenses are great. Elinor forced herself to comment on his expenses, but made sure to remind him that his income was substantial. John disagreed: others might assume his income is large, but it actually isn't. They can live comfortably, however, and he does not mean to complain to her. John tells Elinor about his recent purchase of a farm, which he felt he had to buy. It cost him a lot of money. He also complains that he has had to buy linen and china for Norland after the originals were left to Mrs. Dashwood. Elinor could only comment that she hoped there were easier times for him in the future. John revealed there was work to be done on the garden, yet, so he wasn't sure when their budget would ease up. Elinor was pleased that Marianne was not present for this particular conversation, especially when he revealed that the walnut trees would be torn down to make room for a greenhouse. John was pleased that he had made his poverty clear enough and moved onto another conversation. He complimented Mrs. Jennings on her house, way of living, and her good income, and is pleased Elinor has a valuable friend like her. He assumes she has a fantastic deal of money to leave and suggests that she might leave some to the Dashwoods, but Elinor assures him that what she does have has been left to her own children. It is more likely that she will leave the money to her own daughters than to the Dashwoods. John argues that her daughters are well married and do not need the money. Mrs. Jennings has spent a lot of time and energy on the Dashwoods, so it only makes sense to John that she would leave them money. Elinor tells John he is too anxious for their welfare. John asks what is wrong with Marianne as she has lost weight. He thinks she might be ill. Elinor tells him she has been unwell for several weeks. John thinks that this is unfortunate. Marianne has lost her healthy, beautiful look, and he does not think she will marry well now. He and Fanny thought she would have better prospects in marriage than Elinor, but they have changed their minds now after seeing the change in her. John insists that he and Fanny want to be the first visitors to Elinor when she becomes Brandon's wife. Elinor tried to deny there was any understanding between them, but John expected it and could not be persuaded otherwise. It was John's way to atone for neglecting the Dashwoods. If he saw them married well or looked after by Mrs. Jennings he did not have to feel guilty for denying them money.

The meeting with Lady Middleton and Sir John went well, and John went away happy with both of his new friends. He thought Fanny would be delighted with them, too, especially now that John could assure her of their worth in society.

Chapter Thirty-Four

Fanny had enough confidence in John's judgement of Mrs. Jennings that she visited the next day. She found that Mrs. Jennings and her daughters were charming people. Lady Middleton was also impressed with Fanny; they both shared cold, selfish personalities. However, Mrs. Jennings did not approve of Fanny. She thought Fanny was a proud woman who had no affection for the Dashwood sisters and said hardly anything to them. Elinor wanted to ask if Edward was in town, but nothing would prompt Fanny to say his name until she could report that his marriage with Miss Morton was settled, or that Elinor was engaged to Colonel Brandon. Elinor's need for information about Edward came from another person: Lucy. Lucy wanted Elinor's sympathy because she could not see Edward even though he had arrived in London with his brother and Fanny. He did not dare to come and see her himself for fear of being caught, so they could do nothing but wait. Edward visited the house twice while the Dashwoods were out. Although Elinor was pleased he had stopped to visit them, she was even happier that she had missed him.

John and Fanny were so impressed by the Middletons that they decided to throw them a dinner. The Dashwood sisters, Mrs. Jennings and Colonel Brandon would be there, too. They would finally meet Mrs. Ferrars at the dinner, but Elinor did not know if either of the Ferrars brothers would be there. Elinor was happy she would be meeting Edward's mother without feeling an overwhelming anxiety. She could judge Mrs. Ferrars without fear of insulting Edward. Elinor was even happy that the Steele sisters would be attending the party. Lucy had always wanted to meet the family and looked forward to making friends with Fanny. Elinor knew that Edward would be invited to the party and would not be able to refuse. It would be the first time she would be able to watch Edward and Lucy together in public, and she did not know how she would be able to bear it. However, her anxiety was for nothing as Edward would not be able to attend the party after all.

As Elinor and Lucy walked up the stairs together on the day of the party, Lucy admitted she was nervous to meet her future mother-in-law. All of Lucy's happiness depends on this one woman, and she was nervous to meet her. Elinor could have suggested that she was Miss Morton's future mother-in-law, but instead assured Lucy that she sympathized with her. Mrs. Ferrars was a small, thin woman with a rigid posture and a sour personality. She did not speak much, and when she did not one word was uttered to Miss Dashwood. She seemed determined to dislike her. Whereas Elinor would have been hurt by this treatment a few months prior, she was not affected by Mrs. Ferrars at all. Elinor was amused that Mrs. Ferrars treated Lucy with kindness. If she only knew about Lucy and Edward's secret engagement, Mrs. Ferrars would have been horrified! Lucy was happy, and Miss Steele was satisfied that she had been, once again, teased about Dr. Davies.

The dinner was a grand one, and Elinor could see no real signs of the poverty John insisted they were in. They were, however, short on conversation. Neither John or Fanny had anything worth saying, but this was normal for many of Elinor's acquaintances. When the ladies moved to the drawing room after dinner, this lack of conversation was much more obvious. The men had filled in gaps in the conversation with talk of politics, breaking horses in and land, but the women only found themselves debating the heights of Harry and William, Lady Middleton's two sons. If both children had actually been there, this debate might have been solved fairly quickly. However, only Harry was present, and the debate went on. Lucy did not want to please anyone too much, and sat on the fence. Elinor offended Mrs. Ferrars and Fanny by declaring William was taller, and Marianne offended everyone by announcing she had no opinion or thoughts on the matter.

Just before Elinor left Norland, she had painted some pictures for Fanny. John pointed these out to Colonel

Brandon. He admired them, as he would have done for anything Elinor had painted. Other people were curious about them, so the paintings were handed around. Mrs. Ferrars asked to look at them, but after hearing that they were painted by Elinor only said that they were pretty without even looking at them. Fanny turned red, which Elinor thought was a sign she was embarrassed for her mother's rude behaviour. She asked her mother again what she thought of them, became worried that she had been too interested in Elinor's work, and then referred to Miss Morton's beautiful paintings. Marianne could not bear their treatment of Elinor. She told Mrs. Ferrars and Fanny off for complimenting Miss Morton's paintings while looking at Elinor's. They should be talking and thinking about Elinor instead of Miss Morton, who is no one to Marianne. Mrs. Ferrars looked angry and told Marianne that Miss Morton was Lord Morton's daughter. John was embarrassed by Marianne's protest, and Fanny was angry too. Elinor was hurt that Marianne had said something—even moreso than how hurt she had been by what Fanny had said. Brandon, however, seemed to only see the good in what Marianne had said. Marianne did not stop there, however. She moved toward Elinor, put an arm around her neck and told her not to be unhappy because of what they had said to her. Marianne then burst into tears. Almost everyone was concerned about Marianne, Brandon in particular, who walked over to them. Mrs. Jennings gave her salts, and Sir John instantly changed his seat to be closer to Lucy and whispered to her what had happened. In a few minutes, Marianne had recovered enough to sit down again. She still looked quite upset for most of the evening. When John had Colonel Brandon to himself, he told him that he was worried for Marianne's health. He was upset that her beauty had disappeared over the last few months, especially as she had been quite attractive.

Chapter Thirty-Five

Elinor was happy that she had finally met Mrs. Ferrars because it meant she was pleased that their two families would not be connected even further. Mrs. Ferrars' pride and bias would have made an engagement to Edward nearly impossible. She was thankful that she did not have to suffer under Mrs. Ferrars' observation. If Lucy had been a better person, Elinor might have even celebrated the situation. As it was, Elinor could not figure out why Lucy was so blind to Mrs. Ferrars' flaws. Lucy thought that Mrs. Ferrars liked her, but Elinor knew it was just because she wasn't Elinor. She didn't truly compliment Lucy at all. If Mrs. Ferrars knew that Lucy was engaged to Edward, her treatment would be different. The next morning, Lucy visited Elinor alone and declared that Mrs. Ferrars liked her. She was happy with Mrs. Ferrars' flattering behaviour. Elinor only thought she had been polite, but Lucy thought she was exceedingly kind to her. Elinor wanted to talk about something else, but Lucy continued on. Elinor pointed out that if they had known about the engagement their treatment of her would have been different. Lucy thought she might say that, but she didn't think there was any reason why Mrs. Ferrars would have pretended to like her. She thinks everything will end well, and that the engagement will be approved. Lucy wondered why Elinor had never mentioned that Fanny was a nice woman, but Elinor had no answer to this. Lucy asked if she was ill because she had not spoken much. Elinor assured her she had never been in better health. Lucy was glad to hear it, but did not think she looked well. She did not know what she would have done without Elinor's friendship. Lucy is also happy that Fanny and the Middleton's got on well, because it means for more visits between the two families in the future. She will be able to see Edward! Lucy continued to talk about Mrs. Ferrars. Lucy was sure if Mrs. Ferrars had disliked her, Lucy would have been able to see it immediately. She knows that if she dislikes someone, she does not make a habit of hiding it. Elinor did not have to reply to this particular comment, because, at that moment, Edward walked in the room.

The meeting was an awkward one. Edward looked like he was torn between leaving the room and walking further into it. This was an encounter which all three of them wanted to avoid, but could not. There were no other people present to save them from feeling uncomfortable, so they had to recover and carry on. Both of the ladies managed to recover from the shock first. Lucy could not be forward with him. She had to uphold the secret. Elinor was anxious for herself, and for him, and was friendly and easygoing with him to make him feel welcome. She would not let Lucy's presence prevent her from admitting how happy she was to see him, and would not be frightened away from giving him the attention a friend was due. Elinor knew, however, that Lucy was watching them both closely. Elinor's treatment of Edward made him feel at ease, and he could finally sit down. Lucy hardly said a word. Elinor spoke the most and told Edward about her mother, and their journey to London—things that Edward should have asked about, but didn't. Elinor also decided to leave Lucy and Edward alone for a few minutes and retrieve Marianne from her room. Elinor waited for several minutes before fetching her. Marianne rushed into the drawing room and welcomed him like a sister might. Edward tried to return her kindness, but could not say what he genuinely felt in front of the others. Marianne regretted that the delight and enjoyment of this meeting was altered by Lucy's unwelcome presence. Edward was the first to speak after they all sat down and commented on Marianne's changed looks. He wondered if London had altered her health. Marianne begged him not to think of her health, but to look at Elinor. All that mattered that was Elinor was well. This comment made Edward and Elinor uneasy, and Lucy extremely suspicious. Edward asked if they liked London, eager to change the subject. Marianne has not enjoyed London at all, but Edward's arrival has made everything better. She suggested to Elinor that Edward should take care of them when they made their journey back to Barton. Edward muttered something under his breath. Marianne was satisfied by his reaction and moved on with the conversation. She suggested that she had much to say about his sister and mother, but could not talk about it in front of Lucy. She wondered why Edward had not been there, and he admitted he was with other people. Lucy suggested that Marianne did not think men should keep their engagements, hinting at her past with Willoughby to try and get some revenge on her. Marianne calmly replied that it was Edward's selflessness and conscience that had kept him away from the party. Edward stood up, then, and announced he had to leave. Marianne was surprised he was leaving so soon. She whispered to him that Lucy would not stay much longer, but Edward could not agree to stay and left. Lucy left soon after. Marianne wondered why Lucy visited them so often, and why she could not see that they both wanted her to leave. Elinor could not reveal Lucy's secret, and so kept quiet. She could only hope that Marianne would not continue to talk or hint that there would be a further connection between the family in the future.

Chapter Thirty-Six

Mrs. Palmer gave birth to a healthy son and heir. Mrs. Jennings wanted to be with Charlotte as much as possible, so she left soon after she was dressed in the morning and stayed there until late in the evening. The Dashwood sisters spent the whole day with the Middletons after they were invited there. They had wanted to stay behind in Mrs. Jenning's house the entire morning, but this was something against everyone else's wishes. They had to spend their house with the Middletons and the Steeles instead. The Steeles thought that they were intruding and taking some of the kindness they thought should have been all theirs. Although Lady Middleton was polite to them all, it was clear that she did not like either Elinor or Marianne. Their presence did not allow anyone to relax. Lady Middleton did not want to seem idle in front of either Dashwood sister, and Lucy was worried about flattering Lady Middleton too much. Miss Steele, however, continued to drop hints that she wanted a full account of the mishap between Marianne and Willoughby, but these were all ignored. She also wanted them to tease her about Dr. Davies, but nothing was said on that subject either.

All of these problems were undetected by Mrs. Jennings, who thought it was lovely that all of the girls were together. She complimented the Dashwood sisters on having escaped the company of an old woman for the day. Whenever she joined them, she was full of compliments and happiness. The only thing Mrs. Jennings complained about was Mr. Palmer's approach to children. She could not persuade him that babies were all different, and he refused to admit that his child was the best in the world. While Mrs. Jennings and the two Dashwood sisters were visiting Fanny one day, another one of her friends had dropped in. This visitor's imagination had led her to believe that the Dashwood sisters were actually staying with Fanny, because her husband was stepbrother to them. She left an invitation for Fanny, John and the two Dashwood sisters for a small musical party at her house. The consequence of this shared invitation meant that Fanny had to send her carriage to retrieve the Dashwood sisters and had to pay attention to them during the party. Marianne had become used to going out every day that she did not mind whether she did go out or not. She prepared for the party assuming that there would be no true enjoyment during it or anyone. She did not even care much about her appearance, either, and barely knew what she had put on. Miss Steele, however, was curious about everything Marianne was wearing. By now, Miss Steele could probably guess the number of gowns Marianne owned, and was probably looking to find out how much her washing cost per week and how much money she had to spend on herself each year. These impolite questions usually finished up with a series of compliments.

The evening was not a unique event. The party consisted of attendees who had taste for great performances, and those who had no taste at all. Elinor was not musical and had no problem with looking away from the performers to glance at a group of young men. The gentleman who had ordered the toothpick at the jewellers was there and was speaking to John. Clearly they knew each other from somewhere, and Elinor was determined to find out who he was. Elinor discovered, after John introduced them, that this was Mr. Robert Ferrars. He addressed them politely, but Elinor could see he was the conceited man he had been described as. Elinor wondered to herself why the two brothers were so different, and Robert just happened to offer his own theory without prompting. He thought Edward did not spend time with the correct people. He also thought Edward did not benefit from a private education. Robert's time at a public school meant he was fit and able to mix with many in the world. He consistently tells Mrs. Ferrars that the damage to Edward was done by her own hand when they placed him in private education. It would have been better to send him to school rather than placing him with Mr. Pratt. Elinor kept quiet. She would not voice any opposition or defense of private education, especially when she could not think of Mr. Pratt's family with satisfaction. This had been the thing that had led to Lucy's engagement, after all.

After a little conversation about the Dashwood cottage, Robert declared that if he had the money to do so, he would build his own little cottage where he and a few friends could gather. He thinks that everyone should build a cottage if they were going to build anything. He argues that even though many might think there is not enough room in a cottage, these people are mistaken. He visited Lady Elliot in a cottage last month. She did not think she had enough room for a dance, but Robert arranged the house so that there would be room. Elinor agreed with him because she did not want to compliment him with her reasonable questions.

John Dashwood did not enjoy music any more than Elinor did, and so he let his mind wander. A thought struck him: the mistake that Mrs. Dennison—the host of the party—had made in believing that the Dashwood sisters were staying with them had raised the question of whether or not it would be polite manners to invite them while Mrs. Jennings was engrossed with Charlotte's new born son. It would not cost them anything more or inconvenience them, and it would fulfil part of his promise to his late father. When Fanny heard the proposal, she was shocked. She did not understand how it could be done without insulting Lady Middleton, as the Dashwood sisters spent every day with them. She claimed to be willing to invite them if they were not Lady Middleton's visitors. John did not understand her objection, particularly as they had already spent most of a week at Lady Middleton's house. Fanny paused for a moment and then announced she had already asked the Steele sisters to spend a few days with them. She felt that they should have attention paid to them, just like Mr. Pratt, their Uncle, did for Edward. They could ask the Dashwood sisters at anytime, but the Steeles might not be in London anymore. John was convinced that they should invite the Steeles over, and his conscience was calmed by this charity. He decided that he would invite them over the following year, while secretly believing that Elinor and Colonel Brandon would be in London the next year as husband and wife, and Marianne would be *their* visitor. John would never have to invite them over.

Fanny was pleased she had escaped the Dashwood sisters and invited Lucy and Miss Steele to their house as soon as Lady Middleton could let them go. Lucy was happy—Fanny was working to secure their friendship, and having time with Edward and his family was in her best interests. While the visit to Lady Middleton had never had an official ending date, Lucy announced that they were always meant to leave the house in two days time anyway.

When Lucy showed Elinor the letter, she agreed that it was evidence that Fanny was not acting purely out of spite to Elinor and seemed to honestly care about Lucy. It suggested that the engagement might have a future after all. The Steeles arrived at Fanny's house, and everything Elinor heard about their visit generally suggested that Fanny had never been more pleased with a pair of young ladies in her life. They had become excellent friends, and Fanny announced she did not know if she could ever do without them again.

Chapter Thirty-Seven

Mrs. Palmer was well enough after two weeks that Mrs. Jennings did not feel she had to give up all of her time to her daughter. She decided to only visit once or twice a day, and spend the rest of the time at her own house to spend time with the Dashwood sisters. After the third or fourth day, Mrs. Jennings returned from the Palmers with a bustle that suggested something important had happened. She asked Elinor if she had heard the news, which she hadn't. Mrs. Jennings had found Charlotte fussing over her son, who had not stopped crying. The baby had pimples and Charlotte was convinced he was ill. A Doctor was sent for and told her that the child was perfectly fine. As he was leaving, Mrs. Jennings asked him if there was any news. He smirked and whispered to her that he hoped Mrs. Dashwood would be well. Elinor asked if Fanny was ill. Mrs. Jennings told her this was the exact question *she* had asked the Doctor. He revealed that Edward was engaged to Lucy, and no one knew about it. Mrs. Jennings could not believe it was true or even possible for no one to suspect them. She suggests that if she had seen them together she might have been able to guess it for herself. Anne, in the belief that the family loved Lucy enough that they would not object to the engagement, told Fanny the news. She started to scream and cry because she had thought just five minutes before that Edward was engaged to a Lord's daughter. Edward heard the screams and went upstairs to see how she was, and Lucy followed. Fanny told them both off, which made Lucy faint. Fanny told them that neither would be allowed to stay in the house, and John begged her to let them stay until they had packed. Fanny dissolved into hysterics, which was when the Doctor was called to help. Mrs. Jennings pitied Lucy, but blamed Fanny and Mrs. Ferrars for believing too much in fortune and status. She did not know why Edward and Lucy could not marry!

Elinor said what she was meant to say in this circumstance, and was glad that she was not suspected of having anything to do with it. As Mrs. Jennings had long given up on the match between her and Edward, she could speak with no bias. Elinor was anxious to hear what Mrs. Ferrars would say and do, and how Edward would react. She was worried for him, but not for Lucy. As Mrs. Jennings would not talk about anything else, Elinor felt she should prepare Marianne. She had to make sure that Marianne knew the truth so that she did not show others that she felt sorry for Elinor or resentment for Edward. Elinor knew she was about to remove Marianne's only hope at the present, and hoped that she would be able to defend Edward. Elinor, although she cried a little, told Marianne the truth without dissolving into violent hysterics. Marianne, however, was horrified and cried much more. Elinor had to comfort Marianne even though she should have been comforted by Marianne. She thought Edward was a second Willoughby. As for Lucy, she could not believe that anyone had wanted to marry her. She did not think it was a natural match for Edward, and Elinor had to leave her to her own beliefs. Marianne asked Elinor how long she had known about the engagement, and she revealed she had known about it for four months. Marianne was shocked—even when she had resented Elinor for being happy, she knew that Edward was already engaged. Marianne did not know how she has managed to remain so calm and happy. Elinor explained that she was doing her duty. She had to be secretive because of her promise to Lucy. Elinor also didn't want Marianne to suffer because of her. She wishes Edward will be happy, even if he does regret doing his duty to Lucy. Lucy does not have any sense, and Elinor feels that this is the foundation that good can be built on. She fears that the marriage will end badly, but Edward *will* marry Lucy and will forget, with time, anyone who might seem superior to her. Elinor does not believe in Marianne's theory that there is only one person they will ever fall in love with It does not make sense to her. Marianne does not think that Elinor has felt much pain in her loss of Edward. She denies this—for four months she has been able to say anything to anyone about her loss of Edward. The knowledge of Edward's engagement was forced on her by the exact person who had ruined all of her dreams. She has then had to listen to Lucy talk about her hopes again and again, and has never heard of anything which might give her hope for her own future with Edward. Elinor has also not heard anything which would make her desire the connection any less than she did before she heard of the engagement. Elinor has suffered while she has tried to maintain a calm, unaffected composure. Marianne was horrified, and cried out that she had been awful to Elinor. While Elinor comforted Marianne through her loss, Marianne has shown no gratitude for it. Now that Marianne was upset enough, Elinor had no trouble getting her to promise to not talk of the engagement with resentment or openly hate Lucy. Marianne did her job well: she was discreet when Mrs. Jennings told her the news and did not blush once. Elinor was proud of her.

The next morning, John came to visit them and tell them the news himself. He told them that Fanny and Mrs. Ferrars had both suffered with distress, but the Doctor thought that they would both be fine. John declares that Fanny has the strength of an angel. She has announced to him that she will never think well of anybody else again considering she had been deceived by the people she was so kind to. Fanny wishes she had invited the Dashwood sisters rather than the Steeles. Mrs. Ferrars asked Edward come and see her and told him to put an end to the engagement. Edward was stubborn enough to refuse. Mrs. Ferrars explained her plans for him: if he married Miss Morton, he would be given the Norfolk estate and a thousand pounds a year. If he stayed with Lucy, he would receive no money from her, and Mrs. Ferrars would do everything in her power to prevent him from finding employment. Marianne declared she did not think this was possible. John, believing she was referring to Edward's opposition, agreed. Marianne stopped herself before she said anything else. Edward told the family that he would stand by Lucy and the engagement, whatever it would cost him. Mrs. Jennings declared that she would have thought badly of Edward had he not stood by Lucy. His actions have made him an honest man, and Lucy is a kind girl who deserves a good husband. John was astonished. He did not mean to offend Mrs. Jennings' cousin, Lucy. He assured her that Lucy deserved a good husband, but the secret engagement was unusual and not what the family wanted for Edward. Mrs. Ferrars has sent Edward away forever. John does not know where he has gone, or if he was still in London. John feels sorry for him and wonders what he will do on his low income. Mrs. Jennings wished she could offer a room in her own home, but no one knew where he was. John stated that Edward might have been able to help himself had he done the thing that was expected of him. The entirety of the Ferrars estate will now rest on Robert. He will be the sole heir. Mrs. Jennings thought that was his mother's revenge, but she would not have done the same. After a few more sympathetic moments, John left them alone.

Chapter Thirty-Eight

Although Mrs. Jennings had declared Edward was noble and honest, only Elinor and Marianne knew how much Edward had sacrificed, and how little he had received in return. Elinor and Marianne forgave him for everything and felt only compassion for him. Although they were forced to listen to the subject in public, in private they wanted to avoid talking about it. Marianne's assurance that Edward still loved her hurt Elinor. They did not hear anything new for a few days. On the third day, Mrs. Jennings and Elinor went to Kensington Gardens. Marianne stayed behind after she heard the Willoughby's were back in London. She did not want to meet them. A friend of Mrs. Jennings joined them shortly after they arrived, and Elinor was pleased that she could sit still and reflect quietly by herself. Neither the Willoughbys, Edward, or anyone of interest to her was present in Kensington Gardens. However, Miss Steele suddenly turned up. She looked quite shy, but joined them after Mrs. Jennings encouraged her to do so. Mrs. Jennings whispered to Elinor to try and get Miss Steele to tell her everything. Miss Steele did not need any encouragement and revealed everything to Elinor.

After Elinor assured her that neither Mrs. Jennings or Lady Middleton were angry with them, Miss Steele declared that Lucy was angry with her at first, but has calmed down since. She even added a ribbon to Miss Steele's hat. She laughs, suggesting that she might only be wearing pink ribbons because they are the Doctor's favourite colour. Elinor had nothing to say on this subject, so Miss Steele wandered back to her first subject. Miss Steele tells Elinor that others have talked about Edward refusing to marry Lucy. Elinor has heard nothing about it. Many ladies were surprised that Edward could give up Miss Morton, especially when she had thirty thousand pounds to her name and Lucy had nothing at all. The family thought Edward might leave them alone and abandon Lucy, and when he did not come to see them for three days they started to believe in these rumours. However, that morning he arrived at the house and revealed that he had refused to give the engagement up and had lost his fortune. He had gone into the country to think for a while and returned to offer Lucy a way out. He did not think it was fair for her to marry someone with no fortune. Lucy would not let him out of the engagement because she thought she could live on nothing if she was with him. They agreed that Edward would take religious orders immediately and must wait until he has a job before they get married. However, at that moment, Miss Steele was called away. She had to go into the room and interrupt them to ask if Lucy wanted to come with her to Kensington Gardens, but she would not leave Edward. Elinor stopped her there and asked how she knew what they were saying if she wasn't in the room with them. Miss Steele revealed she had been at the door listening in. Elinor wished she'd known this before she had told her what was said, or she would have stopped the conversation. She thinks this is unfair to Lucy. Elinor tried to change the subject, then, but Miss Steele would not be stopped. Miss Steele thought Mrs. Ferrars, Fanny and John were all cruel people. She wondered where Edward would end up. Before Miss Steele could continue, the rest of her group of friends approached. Miss Steele suggested that she and Lucy could stay with Mrs. Jennings if the Dashwood sisters left, and then left. Elinor thought about the conversation: it was certain that Edward and Lucy were going to be married, despite the delay until Edward had a job.

When they returned to the carriage, Mrs. Jennings asked for information, but Elinor did not want to repeat everything Miss Steele had overheard without Lucy's permission. Elinor told Mrs. Jennings that the engagement was still on and that they would wait until Edward was earning money. Mrs. Jennings thought if they waited and nothing would come Edward's way they would be poor, with too many children and no furniture. Mrs. Jennings hoped she might be able to help in some way.

The next morning, Elinor received a letter from Lucy which reported both she and Edward were doing well and were happy. They were grateful for her friendship and kindness. She was angry with Anne, but she knew what she did was for the best. Lucy hoped that Mrs. Jennings would come to visit them. As soon as Elinor finished, she handed the letter to Mrs. Jennings—Elinor was sure this was exactly what Lucy had hoped in sending the letter. Mrs. Jennings thought the letter was remarkably well written, and reveals Lucy has a kind and good heart.

Chapter Thirty-Nine

The Dashwood sisters had been in London for more than two months, and Marianne grew more impatient every day to go back home. She longed for the quiet and freedom of the country and knew that being back in Barton would put her at ease. Elinor was also quite anxious to return despite the difficulties of the long journey. However, before Elinor could suggest to Mrs. Jennings that they might go back home, *she* suggested another destination. The Palmers were going to Cleveland at the end of March for a few weeks, and Mrs. Jennings and the Dashwood sisters had received an invitation to accompany them. Mr. Palmer's invitation was so polite, and his manners were so different that Elinor felt she had to accept the invitation immediately. When Elinor told Marianne what she had done, Marianne was upset. She did not want to go to Somersetshire, where she was hoping to go with Willoughby. She could not bear it. Elinor suggested that Marianne see it as a kind of deadline for when they would return home. Barton was only a day's travel away, and their travels would be far more comfortable if they went with Mrs. Jennings. They would not need to stay for more than a week in Cleveland, so Marianne could imagine that they would be home in three weeks time. Marianne's love for their mother overrode any objections she had for this plan. Mrs. Jennings wanted them to come back with her from Cleveland, but Elinor refused on account of their mother waiting for them. She confided in Colonel Brandon one day that she did not know what she or he would do without the Dashwood sisters. Mrs. Jennings' hopes in reminding him of the loss of the Dashwoods in the future were that Brandon would make some sort of move toward Elinor. She was not disappointed. He moved to the window to talk with her quietly. Mrs. Jennings tried her best not to listen in and even moved closer to the pianoforte so Marianne's playing would block out their conversation. Still, inbetween a song, Mrs. Jennings overheard him apologizing for the poor quality of his house. Mrs. Jennings believed that this meant the engagement was set. She could not hear what Elinor said in reply, but she guessed, from lip-reading, that Elinor had no objections. Mrs. Jennings also heard Colonel Brandon declare that something would not happen soon, and Mrs. Jennings had to try hard not to stand up and oppose this delay in their engagement. Elinor declared she was grateful for Brandon, and he left soon after. Mrs. Jennings was surprised that Brandon could leave them so suddenly and without much feeling.

What had actually gone on between Brandon and Elinor was the following: Brandon had asked after Edward, and whether his refusal to break off the engagement with Lucy was true. Elinor admitted it was. Brandon thought those who tried to break up the engagement between two young people were terrible people. Brandon had met Edward a few times and was impressed by him, and as Elinor was a friend of his, he wanted to try and help him. Brandon had heard of a vacancy in Delaford and wanted to offer him the place if he felt it was worthy of him. Elinor was overjoyed. She had considered Edward's position to be a hopeless one, and now there was assurance he would be able to find a job and marry Lucy without any problems. Although Mrs. Jennings thought Elinor's compassion and joy was for an entirely different reason, Elinor's gratitude was keenly and authentically felt. She promised to tell Edward of the vacancy and thanked Brandon with all her heart. Brandon regretted that the house was not large—this statement was one Mrs. Jennings had also overheard and mistaken. Brandon continued: he did not think that the income or home would be suitable for a marriage. Brandon would not be able to do anything else to help Edward, and was sorry he could not help Edward secure his true happiness: to be married to Lucy. He thought the marriage would not take place for a long time. Although Mrs. Jennings thoroughly misunderstood the conversation between Brandon and Elinor, it took place with the same feeling that an offer of marriage might have raised.

Chapter Forty

Mrs. Jennings smiled at Elinor and suggested that even though she did not know what Brandon had said to her, she still wanted to congratulate her and wish her happiness. Elinor thanked her. She thought Brandon was a good man, and thought that not many men have as compassionate a heart as him. Elinor is shocked. Mrs. Jennings thinks Elinor is just being modest—she knew this would happen. Elinor did not think Mrs. Jennings could predict it happening so soon. She knows where she will go to look for a happy couple, and Elinor wondered if that meant Mrs. Jennings would go to Delaford herself. Mrs. Jennings will. She does not agreed with Colonel Brandon about the house being a bad one, and if there were repairs he should have carried them out himself. Mrs. Jennings had to leave, then, and suggested that Elinor would like to tell Marianne about her news. She would, but Elinor makes Mrs. Jennings promise not to tell anyone else about it until she has written to Edward. Mrs. Jennings is confused: she does not know why Edward should be written to, but she assumes that they want him to perform the ceremony. She wonders why the Colonel isn't writing to him, instead, but Elinor assured her that Brandon did not want to be impolite by suggesting his plan to Edward. Mrs. Jennings returned for a moment to suggest that Betty, a lady's maid, might be a good servant. Elinor agreed, not really listening to what she was saying and eager to have a moment of reflection to herself.

Now alone, Elinor had to consider how to tell Edward and what to write in her note. She worried about saying too much or too little and sat debating a while. Edward interrupted her by stepping into the room. He had met Mrs. Jennings outside, who had told him that Elinor wanted to talk to him. Elinor was anxious and confused by his sudden appearance, especially as she had not seen him since his engagement had been made public. She felt uncomfortable for a while, and they both sat down together in mutual embarrassment. Edward could not remember if he had apologized for bursting in the room, so did to break the silence. Even though he was sorry for his behaviour, he would have been sorrier had he not seen Elinor and Marianne before he left for Oxford the next day. Elinor decided to be courageous and get it over and done with. She told him about Colonel Brandon's offer. Edward was shocked, and he could hardly believe it. Elinor suggested that Edward's inability to believe in his friends stemmed from the unkind treatment his family gave him. Edward denied this. He could always and has always seen goodness in Elinor. He owes her everything. She denies this—Edward has done this himself because of his own behaviour and circumstances. Elinor did not even know that the position had come available. Brandon has done all of this by himself. Elinor was so unwilling to acknowledge she had anything to do with this situation that it seemed to make Edward even more suspicious. He thought for a moment and then, with great difficult, complimented Brandon on being a great gentleman. Elinor agreed that he was and that Edward would be thankful to have him as a neighbour. Edward did not answer, but his expression was so serious that it almost suggested he wished to not be Brandon's neighbour. Edward stood, then, and decided to go and see Brandon right away to thank him. He left, and Elinor thought to herself that the next time she saw him, he would be married to Lucy.

When Mrs. Jennings returned home, she had much to say about her visits, but was occupied by Elinor's secret. She asked if Edward accepted her proposal, and when everything might be ready. Elinor did not know how long they would need to prepare, but she guessed two or three months might be enough time. Mrs. Jennings did not know how she was so calm, or how they could wait so long for Edward to receive his orders. Elinor was hugely confused—Brandon's only aim was to *help* Edward. Mrs. Jennings wondered if Elinor thought they only reason he was marrying her was to help Edward. Elinor had to immediately explain what was actually going on, which caused amusement on both sides. Mrs. Jennings was still happy and only had to exchange one piece of happy news for another. Mrs. Jennings was surprised Brandon thought the Parsonage was unfit for a married couple or not large enough, but put this down to him being out of touch with the real world. He was too rich to realize how little people could survive on.

Chapter Forty-One

After Edward went to thank Brandon, he went to see Lucy. Lucy was so happy that she told Mrs. Jennings, who visited her the next day to give her congratulations, that she had never felt happiness like this in all of her life. She and Mrs. Jennings shared their expectation that they would be comfortably settled in the Delaford Parsonage before long. Lucy was also intelligent enough to realize that Elinor was partly responsible for the happy situation, even if Edward refused to give her credit. She declared that she would do anything for Elinor in the future because she thought she was capable of doing anything at all for those she truly cared about. She was also ready to worship Colonel Brandon like a saint.

It had been a week since John had visited them to give them the news of the engagement, and since then the Dashwood sisters had taken no notice of Fanny's condition. Elinor felt it was necessary to pay her a visit. Marianne and Mrs. Jennings both objected to this visit, so Elinor had to go by herself. Fanny did not want to meet with her, but before Elinor could leave, John accidentally came out of the house. He claimed he had been on his way to see her and the others, and invited her in. They walked up into the drawing room to find it empty. Fanny was in her bedroom. He promised to go and fetch her soon because he did not think she would object to seeing her. He wondered where Marianne was, and Elinor gave her excuses. Despite missing Marianne, John was happy that Elinor had come by herself. He wanted to talk to her about Brandon's plans for Edward. John cannot believe Colonel Brandon would be so kind, and thinks that Edward will only have the position until the person Brandon actually wants in the job is ready to take it over. Elinor contradicted him and assured John that, as she was the one to relay the information to Edward, she knew all of the conditions of the offer. John wondered what the Colonel's motive was. Elinor assured him that the Colonel was looking out for Edward and nothing more. John asked her not to talk about the situation in front of Fanny. She had been told the news, and took it well, but did not want to hear about it. Elinor resisted commenting that Fanny only took the news well because it meant her brother had acquired wealth without it affecting her or her children. John told Elinor that Mrs. Ferrars did not know the news; he felt it would be best if she continued to be in the dark about it. Only once they are married will she hear all about it. Elinor wondered why it would be kept from her—if she had cast her son away then she should not honestly care if he did or did not have a job. John suggested Elinor did not understand human nature. When Edward's marriage takes place, Mrs. Ferrars will feel as if she had never sent him away. She will never forget that he is her son. Elinor thinks Mrs. Ferrars has already forgotten Edward, but John insists Mrs. Ferrars is a highly affectionate mother. Elinor said nothing in reply to this.

After a moment, John mentioned that Robert would now marry Miss Morton. Elinor suggested that she had little say in the matter, especially as John seemed to exchange Edward and Robert easily. John did not see what difference there would be as Robert was now considered the older son. He did not think one of them was better than the other. Elinor said nothing. John took her hand and spoke quietly. He told her that he had heard from Fanny that Mrs. Ferrars' objections to Edward's attachment with Elinor would have been smaller than those she had for Lucy. Mrs. Ferrars thought that Elinor was the better match for Edward out of the two of them. Although their engagement was obviously out of the question, John assured her she would still do well for herself. He wondered if Colonel Brandon had visited her lately. Elinor was glad she did not have to reply: they were interrupted by the arrival of Robert. After a few moments, John remembered that he was going to go and fetch Fanny and left the room in search of her. Elinor was left to talk to Robert. He seemed unconcerned about his brother, Edward, and this only served to confirm Elinor's dislike of him.

They had only talked for a few moments before Robert mentioned Edward. He had heard of Brandon's offer and was curious. After Elinor told him the details, Robert laughed. He thought the idea of Edward as a clergyman was ridiculous. Elinor waited in silence and could not stop herself from staring at Robert with surprise. Robert did not notice, however, and actually surprised Elinor by coming to his own senses. He admitted that the situation was quite serious and that he was sorry for Edward. He was not surprised that this happened to Edward, and blames it on his education. He always expected something to happen. Robert was sorry that his mother, Mrs. Ferrars, had to go through it. Elinor changed the subject and asked if Robert had met Lucy. He has for around ten minutes, which was enough for him. She was awkward and without elegance or beauty. He believes she is exactly the sort of girl Edward would fall for. He had offered to speak to Edward and persuade him to break the engagement off, but it was too late for him to interfere by then. If he had had the opportunity, he would have tried his best to make Edward see the engagement was a disgraceful one.

Fanny's entrance into the room stopped their conversation. Although Fanny did not mention Edward at all, Elinor could see the effect it had had on her. She was even kind enough to express concern that Marianne and Elinor were leaving London so soon. She had hoped to see more of them. Elinor thought John was proud of her for saying such an affectionate thing.

Chapter Forty-Two

There was only one more visit between Elinor, John and Fanny. During this visit, Elinor received congratulations that they had managed to find a way to Barton without spending too much money, and that Colonel Brandon would be following them to Cleveland after a few days. Fanny also vaguely invited them to Norland whenever they were in the area, which was a unlikely thing to happen anyway. Many of her friends wished she would go to Delaford to visit Edward and Lucy, and it amused Elinor to think that the one place she would rather not visit was suggested so often as a destination.

Early in April, the Dashwood sisters, Mrs. Jennings, Charlotte and the child all left for Cleveland together. Colonel Brandon and Mr. Palmer would follow after a few days and meet them there. Although Marianne was the most eager out of all of the group to leave London, she could not leave the house without remembering that she had entered it full of hope and joy in her future with Willoughby, and experienced great pain after those hopes were destroyed. She cried as she left. Elinor's reaction to their journey was more positive. She did not have anything overwhelming to think about and was not separated forever from Edward. She was free of Lucy's friendship and was grateful that she had brought Marianne away from London without her seeing Willoughby after his marriage. She looked forward to the peace and quiet of Barton. It would do Marianne's state of mind well.

On the third day, the group arrived at Cleveland. Cleveland was a spacious, modern house on a sloped lawn. It had no park, but its ground were extensive. Marianne was overwhelmed by emotion. She was so close to home, and even closer to Combe Magna—Willoughby's home. After five minutes of being inside the house, she left it again and escaped into the gardens. She looked to the hills in the south-east and imagined she might be able to see Combe Mana from them. She was also happy to be free of London and to have the freedom to take solitary walks in the countryside again. She decided to spend almost every hour of her visit to the Palmers walking outside by herself. Marianne returned to the house just as the others were starting to take a walk of their own. They spent the rest of the morning in the kitchen garden, wandering through the greenhouse and visiting the chicken yard.

Marianne had not expected the weather to change during their stay at Cleveland, particularly as it had been nice and dry when they had arrived. It was a surprise, them, that rain prevented her from going out again after dinner. She would have walked through the cold or damp, but heavy rainfall would not have made for a nice walk. The evening hours were spent quietly. Mrs. Palmer had her child to look after, and she talked with Mrs. Jennings about the friends they had left behind in London, and wondered aloud how far Mr. Palmer and Colonel Brandon would travel that night. Elinor joined in with the conversation, and Marianne—as she often did—found a book to read. Mrs. Palmer's kindness made them feel welcome, and Elinor could forgive her inelegance and impolite behaviour because she was so friendly. Elinor could not, however, forgive Mrs. Palmer for her laugh.

Mr. Palmer and Colonel Brandon arrived the next night to a late dinner. Their arrival gave the conversations in the house a bit of a boost. The rest of the group had run out of new things to talk about because of the wet rain that morning. Elinor did not know how Mr. Palmer would act as every time she met with him he was different. She thought he was quite the gentleman and was only occasionally rude to his wife and her mother. The only thing that prevented Mr. Palmer from being a pleasant person to spend time with was the occasional idea that he was better than them. The rest of his habits were in line with Mr. Palmer's status in society and with his age: he spent mornings playing cards when he should have been working, loved his child but did not want to spend too much time with it, had good manners and kept an irregular schedule. Elinor liked him much more than she had expected to, and she was sorry she could not like him more. Mr. Palmer's rude, selfish behaviour prevented her from liking him unconditionally. It also reminded her of Edward, who was selfless and gentler.

Elinor received news about Edward from Colonel Brandon. He treated Elinor like a confidant and told her about his plans for the Delaford Parsonage. His behaviour while they talked, his delight in meeting with her again after only ten days and his ease in talking to her might have justified Mrs. Jenning's assumption that he was in love with her. It might have been enough to persuade Elinor, too, if she did not know that Marianne was his true favourite. Mrs. Jennings watched Brandon's behaviour, while Elinor watched his eyes. His constant worried looks toward Marianne more than suggested his concern for her health as she seemed to be getting a cold.

Two evening walks all over the gardens in the wet grass, followed by sitting in her wet shoes and stockings, gave Marianne a violent cold. Everyone around her grew more concerned and suggested cures. Marianne refused to take anything for it and claimed that a good night's sleep would cure her symptoms.

Chapter Forty-Three

Marianne tried to assure everyone that she was better the next day. She even tried to prove that she was by following her regular schedule, but Marianne could not persuade the others that she was well, particularly as she was shivering and tired. When she finally went to bed, Colonel Brandon was amazed that Elinor agreed that Marianne only needed some rest. Marianne had a fever and did not sleep well. She got up, insisting that she was fine, but finally confessed that she could not sit up. She went back to bed, and Elinor was convinced that she needed to send for the Palmer's Doctor. The Doctor examined Marianne and, although he was sure she would only need a few days rest to get better, he announced that she had an infection. This serious word sent Mrs. Palmer into a panic because she did not want her child to get sick. Mrs. Jennings also looked quite worried. She had thought Marianne was ill from the beginning, and encouraged Mrs. Palmer to leave with her child immediately. Within an hour Mrs. Palmer, the child and a nurse left for a relative's house. Mr. Palmer promised he would join her there in a day or two, but Mrs. Jennings declared she would not leave Cleveland house until Marianne was better. She wanted to supply her with the tender love and care her mother might have given her.

Marianne felt especially awful because they were meant to have gone home that day. Their return to their mother would have been a surprise! Marianne said little because she was upset that they would have to delay their return, but Elinor tried to keep her spirits up. She did not believe it would be a long delay, and she tried to convince Marianne that this was true. However, she was not better at all the following day. Although Mr. Palmer wanted to stay to be helpful and to prove he was not as frightened as his wife, Colonel Brandon persuaded him to keep his promise and leave. While Mr. Palmer prepared to leave, Colonel Brandon suggested that he might leave too. Mrs. Jennings intervened. As she still believed the Colonel was in love with Elinor, she did not want him to cause her even more anxiety by leaving. Mrs. Jennings told him that he should stay at Cleveland to be useful to her while Elinor was looking after her sister. Mr. Palmer seconded this: he wanted the Colonel to stay so he did not feel like he was leaving the Dashwoods to fend for themselves. Marianne heard nothing about these arrangements. She did not know that she had been the reason for the Palmers leaving. She did not even know Mrs. Palmer had left, did not comment that she had not been seen and never mentioned her name. Two more days passed, and Marianne was still ill. The Doctor, Mr. Harris, visited every day and continued to talk about a speedy recovery. Elinor was hopeful, but the others were not. Mrs. Jennings did not think that Marianne would ever be well again, and Colonel Brandon—who was forced to listen to Mrs. Jennings all day—could not shake the feeling that he might lose Marianne forever. However, on the third day, Mr. Harris announced that his patient was doing better. Her pulse was stronger, and her symptoms were better. Elinor was cheerful. She was pleased that she had not made more of the situation in her letters to Mrs. Dashwood. Elinor began deciding what day they might be able to travel back home. The day that began so cheerfully, however, did not end, as well. Marianne became ill again toward the end of the day. She was tired, restless and uncomfortable. Elinor decided that this was due to fatigue and sent her to bed. Marianne did not sleep soundly, and Elinor decided to sit with her. Mrs. Jennings knew nothing of this change in Marianne and went to bed. Marianne grew worse, and suddenly woke up. She asked if their mother was coming. Elinor hid her fear and encouraged Marianne to lie back down. She assured Marianne that their mother would be there soon and that it was a long way from Barton. Marianne advised that she should not travel via London or her mother would never see her. Elinor was alarmed and checked Marianne's pulse which was lower and quicker than it had ever been. Marianne continued to talk about their mother and Elinor was so afraid that she decided to call for Mr. Harris and send a message to Barton for their mother. Elinor went down to the drawing room to ask for Colonel Brandon's advice. Elinor told him what had happened to Marianne. Colonel Brandon listened to her in silence, and then suggested he would go to Barton to collect Mrs. Dashwood himself. Elinor thanked him. He then went to send a servant to Mr. Harris while she wrote a brief letter to her mother. Elinor was comforted by Colonel Brandon's presence, and hoped that he would do the same for her mother when he travelled with her. Elinor knew she would be in shock; Colonel Brandon would be able to calm her down and keep her company during the journey. Neither of them wasted a moment. Colonel Brandon took Elinor's hand momentarily, and then hurried into his carriage. Elinor returned to Marianne's room to check on her. She watched her for the rest of the night; Marianne spent hours delirious and in pain, and Elinor spent them in extreme anxiety. Mrs. Jennings' servant did not help by hinting to Elinor what her mistress had always thought of Marianne's illness. Marianne continued to call for their mother, and Elinor felt guilty having delayed sending for her. She imagined what might happen if Mrs. Dashwood arrived before Marianne succumbed to her illness, or lost all of her rational mind.

Elinor was just about to call again for Mr. Harris to come when he finally arrived. He did not ease Elinor' mind, and was shocked at the sudden change in Marianne. He insisted that a fresh course of treatment would help Marianne, and then left, promising to call again in thee or four hours. Mrs. Jennings finally heard what had happened when she woke in the morning. She tried to comfort Elinor, but her own heart had lost hope. She was upset that Marianne might die, especially after the months of her misery. Elinor and Mrs. Dashwood's future suffering was also a great concern for Mrs. Jennings. Mr. Harris returned as promised, but was disappointed in the affect of the medicine on Marianne. Her fever had not broken, and Marianne had become extremely quiet. Elinor understood the Doctor's fears all at once and considered calling for more help. Mr. Harris did not think it was necessary and recommended another course of medicine, even though it had not worked the previous time. Elinor was not caught up in his hope this time. She was calm, except when she thought of their mother and how upset she might be. She sat with Marianne until noon, overcome with sad thoughts. Mrs. Jennings suggested to Elinor that the illness was probably brought on by the weeks of misery Marianne had been subjected to. Elinor thought this was a reasonable idea, and it made her even sadder.

By noon, Elinor thought she saw a change in Marianne's condition. She did not dare to voice her hope that Marianne might be coming out of her fever. Instead, she watched and waited, checking Marianne's pulse. Elinor could not take it anymore and told Mrs. Jennings what she thought, but Mrs. Jennings did not want her to get her hopes up. Elinor tried not to let her hopes blossom, but it was too late. Elinor watched Marianne intensely for further changes. Marianne's breath, skin and lips suggested that she had come through the worst of it. Marianne even opened her eyes and looked at Elinor with a more rational gaze. Elinor did not allow herself to believe Marianne was truly well again until Mr. Harris returned and assured Elinor that her sister would come out of her sickness. He declared that Marianne was out of danger. Even Mrs. Jennings, who had been convinced that Marianne would die, believed in Mr. Harris' judgement and cheerfully predicted her complete recovery. Elinor was not happy, but she was satisfied. She stayed by Marianne's side for the rest of the afternoon, watching her every move and calming herself. She was afraid a relapse might happen, but when she saw Marianne fall into a deep and steady sleep in the evening, she was finally convinced that Marianne was cured.

Elinor thought about Colonel Brandon and her mother, and regretted that they were taking so long to get to the house, particularly as they did not know that Marianne had been cured. Elinor left Marianne at seven to have tea with Mrs. Jennings. Mrs. Jennings tried to persuade Elinor to rest for a while, but Elinor did not feel tired enough to sleep and would not leave Marianne alone. Mrs. Jennings walked Elinor to Marianne's room, and then went to bed. It stormed that night but Elinor did not think about it. She was happy: Marianne slept peacefully, and Brandon and Mrs. Dashwood had a pleasant surprise waiting for them. At eight, Elinor thought she heard a carriage approaching the house. As she did not expect the carriage until at least ten, she scarcely believed that there was a carriage and went to the window to see. It was a carriage—a carriage with four horses, which explained their early arrival and suggested Mrs. Dashwood was terrified for Marianne. Elinor tried to keep calm while she thought about her mother's probable despair and dread on arriving at the house. She rushed down the stairs and toward the drawing room, where she saw only Willoughby.

Chapter Forty-Four

Elinor startled at the sight of him, and turned away from him to escape the room. Willoughby asked her to stay for a moment, but Elinor refused. She informed him that his business could not possibly be with her, and that Mr. Palmer was out of the house. Willoughby did not care about the Palmers. He had come to talk with Elinor, and not with him. Elinor was amazed. She told him to hurry, especially when she thought about Colonel Brandon finding him in the house. Willoughby asked if Marianne was out of danger. Elinor hoped she was. Willoughby wondered what Elinor thought about him. Elinor thought he might be drunk: there was no other explanation for his odd visit and manners, and asked him to leave. He could return the next day when he was sober. Willoughby admitted that he had had a drink, but only in the midst of a journey from London that day. Elinor was convinced that he had been brought to Cleveland by a different reason than drunkenness and asked him what he meant by his visit. Willoughby wanted to make Elinor hate him less than she did. He wanted to offer an explanation as a kind of apology. He wanted Marianne's forgiveness. Elinor revealed he has been forgiven by Marianne a while ago. Willoughby thought she had forgiven him too early and would like to give her a real reason to forgive him for his actions. Elinor agreed to listen to him.

Willoughby started by assuring Elinor that he had come to Barton for no other reason to pass his time in a pleasant way. When he met Marianne he was pleased by her. He admits he is shocked with his behaviour. Her interest in him fed his ego and vanity, but he did not care about her happiness. He indulged her without any interest in returning true affection. Elinor stopped him: she did not want to hear anymore. Willoughby insisted that she must hear all of the story. He admitted that his fortune had never been large, and his expenses high, especially when he spent time with richer people. He added to his debt every year, and even though the death of his cousin, Mrs. Smith, was meant to set him free, he did not know when that day would come. He had intended to marry someone with a fortune. Marrying Marianne was entirely out of the question as she had no money. Willoughby admitted that he thought he was in love with Marianne, even though he had no idea at the time that he felt that way. Elinor was touched by this revelation. Willoughby did not think there was a man alive who could resist Marianne, and he was at his happiest when he was with her. Willoughby finally decided to take Marianne aside and justify to her why he had led her on when he was already engaged. However, before he could talk to her Mrs. Smith had discovered something that might have lost Willoughby his fortune. Willoughby assumes Elinor had already heard the rest of the story. Elinor has. She wonders how he will justify his actions. Willoughby tells her to remember who she heard the story from and whether or not it could be biased. Willoughby admits that he has done Marianne wrong, but she is not a saint and reacted without being able to understand him. He has also hurt someone else. Elinor tells him off. She thinks his love for Marianne is a further insult to Eliza. He let himself fall in love with Marianne and enjoy himself at Barton while he ignored Eliza and let her fend for herself. Willoughby had no idea what had happened to Eliza and suggests that she might have been able to figure out what to do herself if she had any common sense. Elinor asks him what Mrs. Smith said to him. She was angry with him; Willoughby thought she would be no matter what she discovered as he had not spent enough time with her while at Barton. She told Willoughby he would be forgiven if he married Eliza. He could not do this, so she dismissed him for forever. That night he thought about what he might do and decided that his fear of poverty outweighed his love for Marianne. He knew he could rely on the person he was to marry. However, he had to have dinner with the Dashwoods that night and needed an excuse to not attend. He also dreaded seeing Marianne at the dinner, so went to see her and left her miserable. He hoped never to see her again.

Elinor asked Willoughby why he visited when a letter would have served the same purpose. Willoughby's pride made him visit, especially when he remembered how dreadful Marianne had looked and how satisfied he had been with himself on leaving the cottage. He will never forget how badly he treated Marianne. Elinor asked if he told Marianne that he would return to Barton. Willoughby was not sure if he did. When Mrs. Dashwood arrived her kindness only tortured Willoughby. He was miserable, but he deserved it. Elinor pitied him, but wanted him to leave. Willoughby only wanted to talk about what had happened in London. Elinor admitted she saw all of the letters that were sent between them. When Willoughby received the first letter from Marianne he was overcome with pain. It only served to assure him that, despite the weeks apart, she was still in love with him and convinced he felt the same way. He had thought that Marianne would not care about him anymore, especially as he had been attempting to convince himself of the same. Willoughby realized he still loved her, but could not break off his agreement with Miss Grey now that everything was settled with her. He decided to avoid them to prevent further meetings and letters. He did not want to seem impolite, watched them leave the house one morning, and then visited to drop off a card. Elinor is shocked. Willoughby goes on to tell her that he kept seeing them around London and frequently had to hide in shops as their carriage went past. He tried to avoid the Middletons as much as possible and any other friends the Dashwoods kept. He bumped into Sir John the day after he stopped at Mrs. Jennings' house, and he asked him to the party that evening which he did not attend. The next morning he received another letter from Marianne—one which made him hate himself even more. He tried to answer it but could not form a sentence. Willoughby had to force himself to be a lover to another woman while his head and heart were full of Marianne. When they met at another party, Willoughby regretted having to hurt Marianne again. He remembers how shocked and pale she looked. Willoughby is thankful that Marianne is out of danger and pities their mother for being put under stress and having to look after Marianne.

Elinor asks Willoughby if he had anything to say about the letter he sent. He received Marianne's letter the day after their encounter at the party. Miss Grey saw the handwriting on the envelope and was immediately suspicious, particularly after hearing rumours about his attachment to a lady at Barton. She had guessed that the lady was Marianne, especially after overhearing their conversation the previous night. She opened the letter to read it, and Willoughby admitted he was glad it made her suffer. However, she made Willoughby reply to the letter by copying sentences she wrote. Willoughby had little choice but to appease her. He regretted not having the opportunity to kiss her letters goodbye or admire the lock of her hair he had carried. Everything was taken from him. Although Elinor felt sorry for him, she had to tell him off for playing the victim. Treating his wife unkindly is impolite and does not make up for what he did to Marianne. Willoughby asked Elinor not to talk about his wife at all because she did not deserve any kindness. His wife knew that he did not love her before they married one another. He asks Elinor if she could forgive him a little more now that she has heard the story from his perspective. She can, but the pain he caused Marianne could not have been worse. Willoughby asks Elinor if she will tell Marianne what he has said so that she can forgive him for an actual reason. Elinor will tell her what she needs to know.

Elinor asks him why he visited and how he heard that Marianne was ill. He ran into Sir John Middleton who actually spoke to him after ignoring Willoughby for two months. Sir John's concern for Marianne and his need to make Willoughby suffer made him tell Willoughby about her illness. Willoughby didn't think Sir John should have told him. He revealed to Willoughby that Marianne was dying due to a putrid fever. He had received a letter from Mrs. Jennings that morning telling him all about it. Willoughby was too shocked by the news to pretend it did not affect him, and Sir John actually pitied Willoughby enough to shake him by the hand. Willoughby did not want Marianne to die still hating him, so he jumped in a carriage and made his way to Cleveland house. Elinor did not answer. She reflected on what she had heard and considered that Willoughby's negative traits and mistakes stemmed from his early independence.

Willoughby announced he would go back to Combe Magna, and then back to London in a few days. He asked if she thought better of him now. Elinor assured him she did and wished him happiness. Willoughby thought happiness was not possible for him now. He was not happy with his marriage, and wondered if Marianne would take him back if he ever had a second chance. Elinor told him off for speaking the way he did, and Willoughby announced he would leave with his dread of Marianne's future marriage. Elinor assured him that he could not lose Marianne anymore than he already has, but Willoughby could not stand the thought of someone else loving her. He starts to hint that her marriage to Colonel Brandon would be awful for him, but stops himself before he says the Colonel's name. After mentioning that he is unable to forgive or like those he has hurt the most, Willoughby almost runs out of the room and leaves Cleveland.

Chapter Forty-Five

After Willoughby left, Elinor was too wrapped up in her sadness and thoughts to even think about Marianne. Before he had visited, Elinor had thought of Willoughby as a worthless man but now she felt regret that he and her family would be separated forever. Elinor knew she was partly affected by Willoughby's infectious personality and his love for Marianne, but it was a long while before she stopped feeling his influence.

When Elinor returned to Marianne, she found her just waking up and refreshed by her long sleep. Elinor was overjoyed. Within a half hour of Willoughby leaving the house, her mother and Colonel Brandon arrived. Elinor ran down the stairs to save her mother from worrying. Mrs. Dashwood had been terrified that Marianne might have already died. She couldn't say anything at all—not about Marianne or to Elinor—and as soon as she heard Marianne was out of danger she was so overcome with relief that she had to be helped into the drawing room. Mrs. Dashwood cried tears of joy, hugged Elinor and took Colonel Brandon's hand to express her gratitude. He shared in their relief in equal silence. As soon as Mrs. Dashwood recovered, she went to see Marianne. Although Elinor wanted Marianne to sleep for longer, as soon as she saw mother and daughter reunited, she was delighted. Mrs. Dashwood announced she would sit with Marianne all night and Elinor would finally go to bed. Even though Elinor had not slept the previous night, she was far too agitated by thoughts of Willoughby's visit that she could not sleep. She was upset that she had judged him harshly before she had heard his side of the story and even pitied Willoughby. She was also worried what the news might do to Marianne. She wondered if Marianne would ever be happy with another, wished that Willoughby might be widowed, and then remembered how much more Colonel Brandon deserved Marianne's hand.

Marianne got a little better everyday. Mrs. Dashwood thought she was the happiest woman in the world. When Elinor heard her say this she wondered if she remembered Edward at all. Mrs. Dashwood knew something that Elinor had not thought about. Colonel Brandon had told Mrs. Dashwood that he was in love with Marianne. Elinor already knew this, of course, and hardly reacted. Mrs. Dashwood was amazed that Elinor was not as happy as she was. She thought she would have picked Colonel Brandon as husband for either of her daughters if she'd actually considered it. Colonel Brandon told Mrs. Dashwood that he loved Marianne during their journey to Cleveland. He did not need any prompting to talk about it, and Mrs. Dashwood thought it might be because he was afraid of losing Marianne. She is astonished that Brandon's love for Marianne had lasted from the moment he first saw her and throughout Willoughby's advances. She is convinced that Brandon loves Marianne more than Willoughby ever did or ever thought he did. Elinor reminded her that they already knew Brandon was a fine man. Mrs. Dashwood thought that his journey to Barton Cottage to bring her to Marianne was further evidence that he is a great man. They further discuss his personality and Elinor reminds her mother that Brandon has consistently been kind to everyone he meets.

Elinor asked if Mrs. Dashwood gave him an answer. She could not have given him an answer then; she was too concerned about Marianne. Brandon had not told her about his love for Marianne because he was hopeful for their future together. He had told her because he wanted to comfort her. Mrs. Dashwood did tell him that if Marianne lived that she would be happy to see them married to one another. Once they arrived at Cleveland and discovered Marianne had survived, she continued to repeat her wishes that they would be married. Brandon, however, thought Marianne would not be able to get over her love for Willoughby. Even if she did, he did not think Marianne would care for him. Mrs. Dashwood thought that they would be the perfect couple—he would be exactly what Marianne needed. Mrs. Dashwood remembers there was something in Willoughby's eyes that she did not like. Elinor did not remember her ever saying anything about it. Colonel Brandon's kind and gentle manners will make Marianne happier than she ever would have been with Willoughby. Elinor did not wholly agree with this but said nothing. Mrs. Dashwood would be close to Marianne as well, and might even move to Delaford to be in the same village as her. Elinor worried about going to Delaford but said nothing. Later, Elinor reflected on the conversation by herself. She hoped that Brandon would be successful, but felt sorry for Willoughby.

Chapter Forty-Six

Marianne's illness was not long enough to make her recovery slow. She was able to move into Mrs. Palmer's dressing room within four days. When she was there, Marianne requested Colonel Brandon visit her. She wanted to thank him for his help. When Colonel Brandon entered the room, it was clear he was emotional on seeing her better. Elinor also thought there was a change in him, and that this was probably because others knew about his feelings for Marianne. She also thought he might be thinking about Eliza, and how similar their sickness had been.

After another day or two, with Marianne growing stronger, Mrs. Dashwood began talking about going back to Barton Cottage. Colonel Brandon and Mrs. Jennings offered the use of a carriage to make sure Marianne returned home safely, and the Colonel was invited back to the cottage in a few weeks. When the day of their departure arrived Marianne actually seemed to feel sorry she wouldn't see Mrs. Jennings for a while. This was probably out of her guilt for not spending more time and effort with her. Colonel Brandon left for Delaford, and the Dashwoods left for Barton. Marianne was well looked after on the journey, and Elinor was glad she was no longer suffering.

When they entered Barton and Marianne began thinking about her past in this place with Willoughby, she grew silent. When Elinor helped her out of the carriage, she saw Marianne had been crying. As Marianne had tried to hide her tears, not draw attention to them to make others feel sorry for her, Elinor felt proud of her. When they walked into their sitting room, Marianne looked around the room as if trying to remember every object in it that had a connection to Willoughby. She did not say much, but what she did was aimed at being happy. Even when Marianne sighed, she followed it with a smile. She went to the pianoforte to play, but the sheet music out on it had Willoughby's handwriting on it. She put the sheet music away, closed the pianoforte and promised to practice more often in the future.

Marianne was much happier the next day. She talked about plans for the future: long walks with her sister, getting up early and practising music and reading. Marianne has decided to improve herself and study new books from the Barton Park library and from Colonel Brandon. Elinor was proud of Marianne. Whereas she had made plans like these in the past and not kept to them, the same enthusiasm seemed to be genuine this time. Elinor remembered that she had not kept her promise to Willoughby yet, and worried what affect it might have on Marianne's peace. She wanted to wait until Marianne was fully healed, but she did not keep to this promise. Two or three days after they had returned home, the weather was nice enough for Marianne to go for a walk. Marianne and Elinor went for a gentle walk together. Marianne pointed to the hill where she had first met Willoughby. She was happy she could talk about that day with little pain, and asked Elinor if they would ever talk about him. Elinor told her to say what she wanted. Marianne does not regret what happened with him anymore. Marianne wishes she knew if he actually felt something for her or was only pretending, or if he was not as evil as others had made him out to be. Elinor asked if she would be at peace if she knew this. Marianne would. Elinor wondered to herself if she should say something now or wait until later. Elinor asks if Marianne compares her behaviour to Willoughby's. She doesn't—she compares it to Elinor's. Elinor reminds her that their situations were quite different, but Marianne tells her to stop being so kind. Marianne's illness has given her time to think seriously. Her behaviour since the previous year had been impolite. She had been unkind to others on many occasions. Her illness had been brought on by her own neglect of her health. If she had died, it would have been her own fault. Marianne did not know what Elinor and Mrs. Dashwood would have done if she had died, especially as Marianne's last days had been selfish ones. She had repaid all those who had been kind to her with selfishness; even John and Fanny deserved more than Marianne had given them. Marianne had insulted her own sister by failing to recognize the amount of pain Elinor had been in, and had even turned away from her. She only thought of her own pain and sadness.

Marianne has decided that she will try to govern and control her feelings and temper to avoid torturing herself or others. She will live only for Mrs. Dashwood, Margaret and Elinor, and will never have the desire to leave her home for another again. If she does go into society, she will only do so to show that she has been humbled and is a gentler person. Marianne will not pretend that she will be able to forget Willoughby, but she will try to control her feelings about him. Elinor decided she would tell Marianne about Willoughby's visit. Marianne did not say a word, began trembling, and she turned pale. She cried as she listened to Elinor, and—although she had many questions—did not say a word. Elinor was worried that Marianne would be ill again and led her back home. Even though Marianne asked no questions, Elinor guessed what she would have liked to know and spared no details. After they entered Barton Cottage, Marianne kissed her, told her to tell their mother and walked upstairs. Elinor went to do exactly that.

Chapter Forty-Seven

Mrs. Dashwood was glad that she could pity Willoughby and wish him well. She could not forgive him and welcome him back as family friend, however. If she had been present when Willoughby told his story, she might have felt more compassion for him. Elinor might have pressed for a kinder reaction to the story from her mother, but time had provided Elinor with perspective, and she only told her the plain facts. That evening, Marianne began to speak about Willoughby again. She turned red and spoke in an unsteady voice. She assured them that she had heard what she needed to hear and did not wish anything was different. She could never have been happy with him, especially knowing that she would have eventually discovered all of his secrets. Elinor congratulated her on her good judgement. If Marianne had married him, she would have been poor financially and emotionally. Willoughby would have always put her second and himself first. Marianne asked if Elinor honestly thought he was selfish. Elinor thought everything he had done suggested it. He played with Marianne's feelings, delayed telling the truth and then fled Barton without telling Marianne the truth. His ease of mind was his only concern. Marianne agreed that her happiness was never one of his aims. Elinor believes Willoughby only regrets his actions because he is unhappy in his marriage. This does not suggest that Willoughby would be happy if he married Marianne. Mrs. Dashwood and Marianne both admit they were foolish. Elinor suggests that all of Willoughby's problems started when he left Eliza to fend for herself. Both Marianne and Mrs. Dashwood agreed. Mrs. Dashwood began to compliment Colonel Brandon, but Marianne appeared to not be listening.

Marianne did not continue to get stronger as she had been over the next few days, but she still tried to appear happy. Margaret returned to the Cottage after visiting others, and the family were once again reunited. Elinor wanted to hear some news about Edward. She had heard nothing about his plans or present status. Elinor and John had sent one another letters to do with Marianne's illness, and the only comment about Edward from him was that they had not heard anything from or about him and assumed he was still at Oxford. One morning their servant returned after running an errand and mentioned to Mrs. Dashwood that Mr. Ferrars was married. Marianne reacted with hysterics. Mrs. Dashwood was shocked, and Elinor turned pale. Mrs. Dashwood did not know which of her daughters to comfort. After making sure Marianne and Margaret were taken care of, Mrs. Dashwood asked the servant who he had heard the information from. Elinor listened on, eager to hear more. The servant saw Mr. Ferrars with his own eyes alongside Miss Steele. He took his hat off to say hello to Miss Steele, who asked about the whole family. She planned on visiting them soon. Mr. Ferrars was in the carriage with her and did not look up or speak. Elinor knew that Edward would never visit them at the Cottage and guessed that they were on their way to Mr. Pratt's. Elinor looked like she wanted to know more, so Mrs. Dashwood asked if she saw them leave. The servant did not, but he did think Mrs. Ferrars looked well. Mrs. Dashwood had run out of things to ask, and the servant left.

When Mrs. Dashwood and Elinor were left alone, they did not say much to one another. Mrs. Dashwood was afraid to say anything. She was upset that she had spent so much time and energy looking after Marianne when Elinor had been suffering just as much.

Chapter Forty-Eight

Now that the marriage was over, and a certain thing, Elinor found that she had always hoped Edward would have remained single—that something would have prevented his marriage to Lucy. Elinor did not think Edward could have received his orders yet, and thought the marriage was quite sudden. She guessed that Lucy must have wanted to get the marriage over and done with without risking any delay. Elinor wondered what Edward might have felt when he saw the Dashwood servant so soon after his marriage to Lucy. Edward and Lucy would soon settle in at Delaford; it was a place that Elinor wanted and dreaded seeing. She imagined them in the parsonage: Lucy would pay attention to their richest friends while turning away from Edward. Elinor thought that a letter would arrive from their friends in London to announce the event, but nothing came after a few days. She did not want to blame anyone, but thought her friends were a little thoughtless.

Elinor asked if Mrs. Dashwood would write to Colonel Brandon. She did last week and expected to see him before she received a reply letter. He would arrive either that day or the next. Elinor looked forward to this—Brandon would have some information for them! Elinor looked out the window and saw a gentleman on horseback stopping at their gate. It was Colonel Brandon, and now she would hear her news. However, Elinor looked closer and discovered it was not Brandon at all, but Edward! Elinor tried to keep calm. Elinor wanted to tell the others not to treat Edward any differently, but she could not speak. They all waited in silence for Edward to come in.

Edward was nervous and afraid. Mrs. Dashwood took his hand and congratulated him. Edward blushed and could not say anything clearly. Elinor talked about the weather. Marianne had retreated out of sight as much as she could to hide her distress, and Margaret kept silent. Mrs. Dashwood put an end to Elinor's conversation about the weather by asking after Mrs. Ferrars. Edward thought she was talking about his mother. Elinor clarified that they were asking about Mrs. Edward Ferrars. Edward blushed, hesitated and then finally told them they meant his brother and Mrs. Robert Ferrars. Marianne and Mrs. Dashwood were shocked. Elinor could not speak but stared at Edward. Edward revealed that Lucy and Robert were married last week. Elinor ran out of the room and burst into tears of joy. Edward saw her run away and became quiet. He left the Cottage without saying a word, leaving the Dashwoods to wonder what had led to this change in Edward's situation.

Chapter Forty-Nine

Although the family could not work out why Edward and Lucy did not marry one another, they at least knew that Edward was a free man. What he would do now was guessed by the Dashwoods: now that he had already entered into an engagement with a woman his mother did not approve of, he could enter into another one without any worries. Edward's errand at Barton was to ask Elinor to marry him. It was odd that he felt awkward asking her the question as he'd already asked someone else prior to this day. No one really knew how Edward managed to pluck up the courage or how he asked: all that was actually known was that they all sat down together about three hours after he arrived. Elinor was engaged to Edward, Mrs. Dashwood approved, and Edward had become one of the happiest men alive. The change in him was obvious, and he now spoke with genuine happiness. Edward revealed everything to Elinor. He confessed his mistakes to her. His engagement to Lucy was a foolish one, and he did not think it would have ever happened if his mother had given him something to do when he left Mr. Pratt's care. He thought he was in love with Lucy, and during the year he was back with his mother he had nothing else to do but focus on his love for her. His brother was not his friend, and he did not like his new friends at all. Lucy was kind to him and pretty. He had few other women friends to compare her too and saw no flaws in her.

The Dashwoods did not think that they would sleep that night—too much had happened! Marianne could not speak, she could only cry. Elinor compared her situation then to what it had been a few hours earlier and knew she was lucky. Edward would stay at the Cottage for at least a week to spend time with Elinor. The subject of Lucy's marriage to Robert was one of the earliest conversations between Elinor and Edward. Elinor could not imagine the two together or how it would have come across. She could not figure it out! Edward guessed that their first meeting led them both to flatter the other and appeal to their vain nature. Edward had no idea how long they had had an agreement for. When he left for Oxford he was only in contact with Lucy, and her letters were not unusual. They came as often and as affectionately as they ever did. When he finally received a letter from Lucy announcing her engagement with Robert, it was a complete and total shock. He handed the letter to Elinor to read. Lucy wrote that she was sure that she had lost his love and had decided to attach herself to another. She was sure that she would be as happy with her new love as she once thought she would be with Edward. She would not settle for someone who was clearly in love with someone else.

Elinor thought Mrs. Ferrars would be very upset with Robert, especially after making him an independent, rich man. After Robert marrying the same woman Mrs. Ferrars had disinherited Edward over, she would be angry and cross. Elinor thought it was an appropriate punishment for her treatment of Edward. Edward thought that she would be angrier, particularly as Robert was her favourite son, but that she would forgive him much faster. Edward did not know how his family had taken the news, or if Robert and Mrs. Ferrars had fallen out. He had left Oxford a day after Lucy's letter arrived with the sole object of getting to Barton. He only wanted to get to Elinor. Lucy's manipulative and mean behaviour had opened Edward's eyes to her real personality and he was thankful for it. He was aware of her ignorance and lack of education, but this was not enough for him to break off the engagement, despite how depressed it had made him. Edward did not know why Lucy had agreed to stand by him when he gave her a chance to break off the engagement. He guessed that she did not think he would be able to make a living in Delaford. Elinor thought Lucy might have hoped something would happen to help them both. She would have lost nothing in continuing with the engagement as it made her look more appealing. Edward understood, then. Elinor told him off for spending so much time with them at Norland and behaving improperly. The whole family were persuaded he and Elinor might have been engaged, only to discover later that he was engaged all along. Edward argued that he believed there was no danger in spending time with Elinor as he was already engaged to another. He told himself that they were only friends and did not realize until later how much in love he actually was with her.

When Edward heard that Colonel Brandon would be visiting the Cottage, he was delighted. He wanted to be better friends with him and to persuade the Colonel that he did not resent the position at Delaford at all. There was one more consideration Edward and Elinor had to make: their incomes. With Edward's two thousand and Elinor's one thousand, they only had three thousand pounds between them. They were not blinded enough by love to know they could not survive on this. Edward hoped that Mrs. Ferrars would change her mind and give him some more money. Elinor did not think Mrs. Ferrars would change her mind at all: Robert's marriage to Lucy might even impoverish Robert and make Fanny richer!

Four days after Edward arrived, Colonel Brandon visited the Cottage. Not all of them could stay in the same house, however, as there was not enough room. As Edward had arrived first, he stayed at night, and Colonel Brandon walked to the Park every night and returned in the morning. Brandon had spent three long weeks at Delaford by himself, wrapped up in thoughts of Marianne. He needed to see Marianne was better to improve his mood, and it did, particularly after Mrs. Dashwood's kindness and compliments. He had not heard about Lucy's marriage to Robert, and their first conversation concerned this subject. Edward and Brandon would have been friends regardless of the situation, but because they were both in love with the Dashwood sisters, it made it inevitable.

Mrs. Jennings wrote to the Dashwoods with compassion for Edward. She was sure he was still at Oxford and heartbroken. She was surprised that Lucy was so cunning. They had sat together for a few hours two days before and Lucy had said nothing at all. Miss Steele had visited Mrs. Jennings in tears as Lucy had borrowed all of her money and left to be married. Miss Steele did not know how she would get back home, and Mrs. Jennings helped her get back to Exeter. Mr. Dashwood's letter was more serious. Mrs. Ferrars and Fanny were suffering quite a bit. They would not be able to forgive Robert, but Lucy's offences were even worse. Neither of their names would be mentioned again to Mrs. Ferrars; if she did end up forgiving Robert, Lucy would never be allowed in her presence. The secrecy of the marriage made the crime even worse, especially as the marriage would have been preventable if others had known. John asked Elinor to join in their regrets that the marriage did not take place. He was surprised that they had not received a letter from Edward. John plans on sending a letter to his brother to suggest a proper letter to Fanny which she could show to Mrs. Ferrars might be an idea. John thinks the kindness in Mrs. Ferrars' heart might lead her to forgive him. Edward decided he would try to reconnect with his family, but would not write a letter asking for forgiveness when he did nothing wrong. Elinor told him he should ask to be forgiven as he did offend them. He could suggest he regretted the engagement to Lucy. If Mrs. Ferrars forgives him, he might then ask her about his second engagement.

Edward decided that it would be best if he went to London to talk to Fanny. Marianne thought that John and Fanny were not entirely bad people if the reunification of the family took place. Colonel Brandon and Edward left Barton together to go to Delaford and look at his future home. After a few nights, Edward would return to his sister and brother-in-law.

Chapter Fifty

Mrs. Ferrars resisted forgiving Edward straight away to prove that she wasn't weak, but after a while she accepted Edward as her son once again. Edward feared that once he announced his engagement to Elinor he might not be her son anymore. He revealed it cautiously, and Mrs. Ferrars listened to him calmly and then tried to argue that Miss Morton would be a better match. When Mrs. Ferrars realized that Edward would not be guided by her arguments, she decided to learn from the past and accept the engagement. Mrs. Ferrars gave them some money so that they would be able to afford to live in Delaford, and the only thing left to do was to make sure the house was ready. Brandon was in the middle of making improvements to the house—especially now that Elinor would be living there—but the work was moving slowly on account of the workmen. Elinor announced that she would not wait to be married, and the ceremony took place in early Autumn. They spent the first month of their marriage with Brandon where they could watch over the improvements to the Parsonage. Edward and Elinor had nothing else to wish for, aside from a marriage between Brandon and Marianne.

John and Fanny visited them at Delaford. He was not disappointed by the marriage, but would be happier if Colonel Brandon would marry Marianne and become their brother. Everything about Colonel Brandon is respectable. He suggests that Fanny should invite both Marianne and Brandon to stay with them as it might encourage them to enter into an engagement. Mrs. Ferrars visited them, too, and did not reveal her true opinion of the pairing while she was there. Robert and Lucy had already managed to gain her favour back. Robert had visited Lucy just after her engagement to Edward was revealed and his only aim was to persuade her to break it off. Lucy suggested at the end of every conversation they had that one more might convince her to break the engagement. Soon their conversations concerned Robert rather than Edward, and it became clear to Lucy that he had taken Edward's place. Robert was proud of tricking his brother and of marrying secretly without needing his mother's approval. They went to Dawlish for a few months, where Robert drew up plans for a few cottages, and then returned to London to regain Mrs. Ferrars' affection and forgiveness. Over time, Lucy had become as necessary to Mrs. Ferrars as Fanny or John were. They had settled down in London, received a lot of financial help from Mrs. Ferrars and were on good terms with the whole family. It was curious that Robert did not care about Edward's low income when he had done nothing to lose it, but Edward was happy with his wife and his home.

Mrs. Dashwood and the Dashwood sisters visited Elinor often. Mrs. Dashwood wanted to see Elinor, but she also wanted to improve the relationship between Marianne and Brandon. Instead of staying with her mother forever and dedicating herself to her studies, she married Colonel Brandon and became the patroness of a village. Brandon was as happy as he deserved to be. Marianne was as devoted to Brandon as she had been to Willoughby at one time. When Willoughby heard about the marriage, he suffered. His punishment came when Mrs. Smith forgave him and suggested that, had he acted with honour towards Marianne, he might have been a happy and rich man. He did not flee society or die of a broken heart. In fact, he lived to enjoy himself. He did, however, believe that Marianne was the most perfect of all the women he had met. Mrs. Dashwood stayed at Barton Cottage where Margaret had finally come of age to start dancing. Sir John and Mrs. Jennings were thankful, especially after the loss of Marianne! Marianne and Elinor lived happy lives and, even though they lived close to one another, did not have disagreements and their husbands remained friends.

About BookCaps

We all need refreshers every now and then. Whether you are a student trying to cram for that big final, or someone just trying to understand a book more, BookCaps can help. We are a small, but growing company, and are adding titles every month.

Visit www.bookcaps.com to see more of our books, or contact us with any questions.

Made in the USA
Middletown, DE
09 August 2017